# Love of the Hunt

# Love of the Hunt

A lifetime in pursuit of deer, elk,
bears, waterfowl, and upland birds

John Winsor

THE LYONS PRESS
Guilford, Connecticut
An imprint of The Globe Pequot Press

The Lyons Press is an imprint of The Globe Pequot Press.

Printed in the United States of America

Designed by Compset, Inc.

10 9 8 7 6 5 4 3 2 1

Library of Congress Cataloging-in-Publication Data is available on file.

ISBN: 1-58574-387-9

To my wife, Tish, who shares my love for the outdoors and has provided forty-six years of enthusiastic support for the pursuit of my passion. Thanks for putting up with me during the time it has taken to research and write this book.

It's also dedicated to my children, John, Susan, and Tom, who have enriched my life by sharing the wilderness with me.

I hope this book will help my grandchildren and future generations understand that man exists because we are a part of the sacred circle of nature.

We reached the old wolf in time to watch a fierce green fire dying in her eyes. I realized then, and have known ever since, that there was something new to me in those eyes—something known only to her and to the mountain.

Aldo Leopold
*A Sand County Almanac*


Our roots go deep, very deep, and it takes only an expedition after game to bring them to consciousness.

Sigurd F. Olson
*Of Time and Place*

For a Book Group Discussion Guide,

to order copies of *Love of the Hunt* for friends,

or share your thoughts, comments, or outdoor stories,

contact the author at

Love of the Hunt@aol.com

# CONTENTS

# ACKNOWLEDGMENTS

A lot of folks contributed to the writing of this book.

Renate Wood kindled my creative spirit after the Yellowstone fires.

Bob Morgan, friend, fellow writer, and lover of nature, gave me the encouragement and criticism that helped elevate these stories to appeal to all readers who share my passion for the wilderness and wild things.

Jerry Mason, who shared many of my adventures, contributed many suggestions, criticisms, and ideas.

Kathleen Phillips provided constant encouragement, critical editing, and good natured patience.

Ken Barrett, for his encouragement and ideas.

Claude and Sue McMillan provided important suggestions.

Thanks to Charlie Butcher for his endless optimism and encouragement.

The gang at Barbara Steiner's critique group helped me find my writing "voice" (whatever that is) and encouraged me to write this collection of wilderness experiences.

Thanks guys.

# CHALLENGED

I'm awakened by a scream. The down quilt falls away as I jerk upright. I stare out the open double doors of my cabin into the black night. High above, cold pinpoints of light make the dark seem darker. Are my goose bumps caused by the cold or the scream?

Below the window the river tumbles over boulders. I strain to hear over the noise of the current. Something is out there, yet I hear nothing but rushing water; see only stars and darkness.

I fumble for my reading glasses on the bedside table. They clatter to the floor. I squint to bring the phosphorescent glow of the clock into semi-focus. It's 5:20, an hour before sunrise.

*E-e-e-e-Wow!* I barely hear the call of a cow elk. Then that high-pitched scream again, the bugle-like call of a bull elk hot in rut. I toss off the covers. My feet hit the ice-cold wood floor. I shiver.

1

He screams again. No, not just any bull elk. It's him. I know his voice, that high-pitched scream that ends in a series of grunts. The same bull I've hunted for the past three years. The same one that makes me walk a hundred miles through the mountains each September. The same guy who allows me within seventy yards two or three times each fall, gives me a glimpse of his antlers through evergreen branches, then disappears in the morning mist.

Last Wednesday morning I found him about six miles north of the ranch, high up on the benches in a pocket of thick timber. I crept so close that I heard him hiccup while he peeked at me through golden aspen leaves.

Under the bed my dog, George, rolls over and sighs, wondering why I'd disturb him in the middle of the night. I can't turn on the lights; they might spook the bull. I grope in the darkness for my underwear, balance on one foot then the other while I pull it up, only to discover that it's on backwards.

He screams again. I feel my way down the split-log stairs and into the mudroom where I keep my camos. Long-john top, shirt. Button it wrong, re-button. Pants, socks . . . where the heck are my socks? In the clutter on the floor, I feel boots, tennis shoes, hip boots. My fingers find the socks. Hip boots, coat, arm-guard, pack, bugle and cow-calls, binoculars, and longbow. Better fill my water bottle; packing out a bull elk is hot work.

I stumble toward the kitchen, bump into the floor lamp next to the leather couch in front of the fireplace where embers still glow. Find the sink, unscrew the top of my water bottle, splash water over my hands. Better take my camouflage gloves. Finally find the neck of the bottle and fill it. Walk past the microwave, where the green glow of the clock says 3:32 A.M.

Three-thirty-two? Naw. Can't be. Stumble to the table where I keep my spare glasses and return to the microwave clock, still 3:32 A.M. I've misread the bedroom clock.

Jeeze! I laugh, then head back to the mudroom, undress, climb the stairs to my bedroom, listen to George fart, slide into frigid sheets, pull the quilt up tight under my chin and shiver. And wait.

He screams again.

Awake and wired, I listen to him scream every twenty minutes or so until it's finally 5:30. This time I put on my reading glasses before looking at the clock. I jump out of bed and start the process over again.

The light westerly breeze is perfect. I'll walk a half a mile upriver, cross it, and climb into the tree stand I built two days ago, then use my call to sound like a horny cow elk. Rut-crazed, he'll rush to find me. My arrow will fly to its mark, and it'll be elk tenderloin tonight. I'll open a nice bottle of Merlot, and even if I'm alone, I'll put a tall red candle on the table, light it, then turn the lights low and savor my victory.

Sagebrush tugs at my feet. I can make out the tiny silver leaves in the starlight, but still can't see ten feet ahead of me. I steer by one bright star hanging over Pilot Peak and keep the sound of the river on my left shoulder. I think about the recent story in the *Cody Enterprise* about a grizzly mauling a hunter. Stop and listen. For what? The bugle of the bull elk . . . or the snapping teeth of a griz?

I climb through the buck-and-rail fence, careful not to let my bow or elk bugle bump; the sound would spook him. The path down the hill to the river is full of loose rocks. I place one foot down, slowly increasing pressure until I have silent, firm footing, then another, and another. It's slow going. I fight the temptation to hurry.

His scream is far to my left. I'm downwind. Perfect. He can't scent me.

My right rubber hip boot slips into the river, then my left. Keeping my feet under the surface eliminates splashing. Slowly now.

Ice-cold water trickles from my calf to the bottom of my sock in my left boot, then I feel a leak in the right boot. Should've bought a new pair. Should've worn wool socks instead of these darned cotton ones. Gonna be cold sitting in that tree.

The far bank is waist high. Like an otter, I slide up and roll over, strip off my hip boots, wring out my socks, and put on my leather hunting boots. I know why that darned bull always smells me. Should've bought new hunting boots, too.

At the base of a spruce tree where I've built a stand, I tie a rope to my bow, clamp the end between my teeth, feel for hand-holds, and climb. Twenty feet up, I can barely see the meadow below, it's still too dark to shoot. I pull up my bow and untie it. I'm not going to rope myself into the tree like I usually do; I don't want to be encumbered in case I have to move fast. Guys fall out of tree stands all the time, but I won't fall. If I do, I won't get hurt. Too badly. I hope. I nock an arrow, wait, and listen.

The river level has fallen since I built the tree stand. There's a riffle behind me that makes hearing difficult. The bull sounds farther off. I wait until I can see across the meadow, then raise the elk cow call and blow the sexiest *E-e-e-e-e-Wow* I can imagine. Heck, I'd come running. So will the bull. Got to be alert, he might come in silently.

I watch, listen. No sound but rushing water. The black outline of a great horned owl cruises past on silent wings. I wait. Finally, it's light enough to use my binoculars to scan the meadow. I search. No elk. I listen. A bugle in the distance. The noise of the water distorts the sound. I can't tell if he's pushed his cows upriver or climbed the bluff toward the swamp. It's senseless to sit here.

I climb down from the tree stand. It's light enough to see the trees across the meadow, but I can't make out the details in the shadows. I weave through lodgepole pines on the meadow's edge, wondering where he's going to take his cows to bed down for the day. He could either head upriver into the wind, or cut up into the partially open rocky ridges, then bed down in the timber several miles downriver.

If I climb a hill about a quarter of a mile upriver, I'll be away from the noise of the current and high enough to hear any sound in that part of the valley.

By the time I reach the top of the hill and bugle to locate the bull, the visibility is better. I listen to the shrill echo of my bugle and wait for the bull, thinking I'm a competitor for his harem, to challenge me. Nothing. I wait ten minutes before retracing my route and climbing through downed timber toward the swamp.

The swamp, still in shadow, consists of tall yellow grass, surrounded by dark timber, hills, and rocky outcroppings. High above, the volcanic cliffs of Squaw Peak are awash in the golden glow of the rising sun. I feel insignificant.

I try a shortcut across a finger of the swamp. My legs sink into frigid water, so I back up and walk the long way around, following a game trail through spruce and downfall. I stop and bugle. Before the echoes of my call die, he screams. The ferocity of his challenge makes me shiver.

Thirty yards to my left, on the edge of the swamp, is a clump of four closely spaced trees. A giant spruce has been toppled by the wind and lies directly in front of them, making a perfect ambush spot. My every sense is directed to creeping into position in the middle of the trees. I pull my camo head net down; only my eyes are exposed.

He screams another challenge. Closer. I take an arrow from my quiver, feel its edge and nock it on my long bow. My feet feel for silent, firm footing. My arm inches the bow into shooting position to check for branches that could ruin a shot.

A ray of yellow sunlight slants through a crevice in the rocky bluff behind me and slices the air about four feet above the swamp. It highlights the white tines of the great bull's antlers, still about a hundred and fifty yards away; his body is hidden in a depression. Like an actor seeking the spotlight, he climbs into the sunlight and stands directly in front of me. I suck in my breath.

He bellows. The vapor of his breath forms a halo that rises slowly through his massive rack. I count the points on his antlers; six on the left, seven on the right.

Silent, bow ready, I watch. He turns broadside to me, screams again, then lowers his head, digs up a wheelbarrow's worth of swamp grass and tosses it high over his shoulder.

My mind replays a video I've seen that shows a bowhunter being attacked by a sex-crazed bull elk. I scan the nearest spruce for hand-holds. There's a stout branch high on the left. Another two feet above it. Then, even higher, one on the left, but it'd be a tight squeeze for my shoulders. Nothing low for my feet. It'll have to do.

Stiff-legged, the bull walks closer, yet not close enough to risk a shot. He turns to his left. Massive body. It's easy to miss if you aim at the entire body. Concentrate on one hair, pick one hair. His antlers strike the ground and toss up another pile of dirt and grass that drifts earthward in the sunlight.

I feel a breath of air on the back of my neck; wind shifting. The vapor of my breath rises in front of me and drifts upward, toward the bull. My scent will rise above him . . . I hope.

He searches for the challenger. One choreographed step at a time, he takes nine cautious steps closer. Another nine and he's mine. I begin to hyperventilate then concentrate to slow my breathing. My lungs won't listen to my brain. Finally, my brain wins.

The bull looks directly toward me. My camo blends with the spruce. He searches the trees to the left, to the right, then raises his head and stretches his dark-maned neck forward. His scream is so violent that his body spasms. He urinates over his front legs in a gesture of male aggression. His bellow is followed by a series of grunts. I feel each hair rise on the back of my neck.

I've been frozen in one spot for how long—hours or minutes? My left leg complains. A cramp coming? My brain calls my hamstring to tell it to relax. It doesn't answer.

The vapor of my breath rises and drifts toward him. The bull's nose jerks high, his nostrils twitch. His tongue snakes out and wets his nostrils.

He grunts and spins. His antlers lay back over his hips as he runs stiff-legged across the swamp.

I fumble for my elk bugle and give a blast with the fighting cow call whose maker claims that it will attract any bull . . . bull.

Bathed in sunlight, he trots up a rocky spine and stops broadside between two ancient lodgepole pines and looks toward me. He raises his head and screams, then begins hiccuping an alarm to his cows, who must be hidden on the other side of the ridge.

I watch my bull and listen to him hiccup until he disappears over the crest, then I walk through golden-topped aspens toward my cabin. I stop to sit for a while on the bluff that overlooks the river valley. Warming in the sunshine, I smile; it's been another great hunt.

# THE BEGINNING

"Let's get ourselves a griz!"

"Huh?" The puzzled look on Don Trieschmann's face delights me. We're best friends, had been co-captains of our undefeated high school football team in 1954, and had wrangled our way onto the school's citizenship ranking committee. That guaranteed us a weekend off campus each semester when Don and I could raise a little hell—mainly trying to get laid, a frustrating, unfulfilled goal. Now we're college sophomores looking for a new challenge.

"Let's go bear hunting. It'll be a blast!"

"That's a pun." Don grins.

"There's this terrific guide, Roy Hargreaves, up in British Columbia. I read about him shooting a world-record Stone sheep in *Outdoor Life* and—"

"They actually shoot sheep?" Don looks bewildered.

"Yeah, wild sheep, but we're gonna shoot a griz, the meanest, the smartest, the toughest beast in the Americas. I've written a couple times to Roy. He wrote back, said he retired, but I told him that everyone thinks he's the best and we'd like him to teach us, but we don't have a lot of money. Guess what? He agreed to take us bear hunting next fall."

"How much?" Don asks.

"Five hundred bucks." I smile at the thought of standing, smoking rifle in hand, over a huge grizzly bear.

"Are you crazy? I don't have five hundred bucks." Don shakes his head.

"Neither do I, but it's December, and we'll get some jobs to earn the cash by the hunt." Nothing will get in the way of my dream.

In May, I send out notices for my new grass-cutting service and am swamped with customers. I hire another buddy, and we scalp lawns all summer. I clear almost a thousand bucks by the middle of August. Don does well doing odd jobs and also has enough cash. We're on our way to hunt griz.

Two weeks later, on the first day of September 1956, our Canadian National Railroad train snakes through the Canadian Rockies.

"Wow! Look at that!" Don points out the window.

I look at a river crashing over boulders the size of houses below the rugged mountains, and I don't feel as tough as I felt when I boarded the train in the flat Midwest. The phrase "Cut down to size" creeps into my mind, but I don't mention it to Don. Maybe the mountains don't affect him this way.

The porter taps me on the shoulder. "Time to get your gear on the platform at the rear of the car. We'll be at Mount Robson in ten minutes."

Don and I throw our duffels over our shoulders, grab our rifle cases, and weave down the aisle to the platform between the cars.

"Wonder how big Mount Robson is? Maybe we can get a beer." Don grins.

"I'll bet it's pretty small, but even small towns have a bar," I say.

We gather at the platform between cars as the train slows. I stick my head out the window, and all I see is wilderness. The station must be around the next bend in the tracks, I think, or maybe on the other side of the train.

The train crunches to a halt.

"Here's your stop, boys. Mount Robson." The porter opens the door, steps off, and we toss him our duffels and rifle cases.

I stand below a railroad sign on top of a steel post that proclaims "Mount Robson."

"Where's the station?" I ask.

"This is it." The porter points to the sign and laughs, then he waves to the engineer and swings aboard the train as it lurches forward. He nods at us, shuts the window, and disappears. We hear the rhythmic swishing of the passing railroad cars as the train picks up speed. The caboose passes, and we watch the train recede until it's a tiny speck against the mountains, then it disappears around a bend.

We stand next to our pile of baggage, alone, in the silence of the wilderness.

"Now what?" Don asks.

"Guess there's no town, but look at that." I point to a rutted dirt road that dead ends at the tracks in front of us.

"No bar. No guide, either." Don sits on our duffels.

"He'll show up." What if I'd gotten the wrong arrival day? Or Roy forgot we were coming? Or something else is screwed up? My stomach knots.

A few minutes later my spirits lift at the sound of a motor. We watch a pickup chug up the dirt track toward us.

"Jeeze, how old is that thing?" Don asks.

The man driving looks just as ancient, must be sixty or seventy. I can tell he's tall and lean. The part of his face that I can see under his wide-brimmed cowboy hat is weather-beaten and hawk-shaped. He pulls to a stop and looks out the window at us with black predator eyes. Over a hand-rolled cigarette in the corner of his mouth he says, "Pile your gear in back and get in."

No hello or howdy or introduction. He's gotta be Roy Hargreaves.

We pile into the bench seat next to him and introduce ourselves. He nods, forces the gear shift into reverse, backs up, turns around, and bumps down the dirt road in silence.

Don and I shoot each other a look. We'd been told that cowboys are sorta quiet. He's gotta be Roy, but I hope not.

A half hour later we pull into his place, which consists of a barn, sheds, and corrals, old and weather-beaten but in good repair. His log cabin is nestled into the sunny side of a hill.

"What's that for?" I asked, pointing to a pipe that runs off the hillside into the wall of the cabin.

Roy looks at me like I'm stupid, then says, "It's our water supply from the spring on the hill. Comes down into a reservoir on the wood stove. That way we have hot water, year around."

"Oh." I hadn't thought about things like plumbing in the wilderness.

"You'll find a bedroom in that shed over there. Stow your gear then come to the house. Supper'll be ready."

We haul our duffels and rifles to the bedroom and test the handmade log beds.

"They feel comfortable," Don says.

"That's a surprise," I respond, referring to our uncomfortable reception.

"That guy's Mr. Personality."

"Probably just takes some time to warm up," I reply. I hope so.

At supper, served by a quiet Mrs. Hargreaves, we meet Roy's daughter and son-in-law.

"They're coming as camp cook and guide," Roy announces.

We listen as he instructs them about what to pack, which horses to take, and other details.

"Only take one camp stove. We'll pick the other one up for the boys at the head of Camp Creek, where that damned jug-headed packhorse blew up last year. Put the stove in the crotch of a tree."

When Roy stops talking, everyone concentrates on their meal. Don and I keep our heads down and shovel in fried beef with boiled potatoes and vegetables from Mrs. Hargreaves' garden.

Roy takes a last swig of coffee and tosses his napkin on the table. "Okay boys, let's go bear hunting."

"Now?" I ask. He'd just been talking about a pack trip.

"Neighbor's got problems with bears eating up his oat field. We're going to shoot a black bear."

"I thought we were here to hunt grizzlies," I venture.

"Going to get rid of a pest, first. Get your rifles and meet me at the truck."

There's a small mixed-breed mutt waiting for us in the back of Roy's pickup. I try to pet him, but he bares his fangs and growls. A lot like Roy.

The truck bounces a few miles to the neighbor's oat field where Roy stops and kills the engine. Without a word, he starts glassing the field.

Don and I scramble for our binoculars and scan the field for bear. I'm looking for a bear standing on all fours, or maybe his hind legs.

"There he is. Middle of the far edge of the field," Roy says, without lowering his glasses.

"Oh, yeah. I see him, just his head." Don is excited.

I finally spot the bear blissfully sitting on his butt surrounded by golden oats. He stretches his paws wide, gathers a bunch of stalks to his chest, and delicately nibbles off the heads. Looks pretty innocent to me.

"Let's kill the son-of-a-bitch!" Roy steps out, opens the tailgate, and the mutt jumps out.

"Uh, how're we going to stalk that bear?" I ask, loading my Remington 30–06 automatic.

"Follow me." Roy leads a fast pace around the corner of the field and marches directly toward the black bear, who flees into the woods when he hears us.

"Get him, Mac!" Roy shouts.

The mutt takes off barking after the bear, and without a word, Roy runs through the forest after his dog.

Don and I look at each other, then start running after Roy.

"He's your bear, Don," I shout.

"Okay!" Don uses his football game voice.

I feel ashamed to set my buddy up so he has to give me the first shot at a griz, but then the trip was my idea.

Roy's out of sight so we crash through the forest after the sound of the mutt, whose barking has changed to a frantic pitch.

"Over here, goddammit. Hurry!" Roy's chainsaw voice cuts through the pine trees.

We find Roy, .22-caliber High Standard pistol in hand, standing under a tree staring up at a black form in its branches. Mutt tries to claw his way up the tree after the hapless black bear who looks down upon all the commotion.

"Shoot him! Shoot him!" Roy shouts.

Excited, nervous, perplexed, and in spite of my pledge that this is to be Don's kill, I raise my 30–06 in concert with Don's rifle. We pull our triggers and blow the bear out of the tree.

Mutt attacks the dead bear while Roy looks at us and shakes his head.

"Didn't need all that fire power. Coulda killed him with this little pistol."

I look at the mutt "wooling" the bear, and I'm flooded with sorrow for the bear, yet thrilled by the chase. My excitement is dampened by Roy's attitude. He seems to have no respect for the bear, no respect for us.

Don's face reflects sorrow while we watch Roy skin out Don's first big game trophy. Soon we're looking down at its skinned carcass.

"It looks just like a human," Don whispers.

"Yeah, guess so." I turn away. We don't talk about our feelings on the way back to the ranch, or later. We're twenty, it wouldn't be manly.

The next morning our packstring pulls out of the ranch. Roy and son-in-law lead the packhorses, Don and I follow the last packhorse, while daughter follows us.

I imagine Roy told her, "Follow close behind them two boys and pick 'em up when they fall off!"

We ride under a blue sky through tall pines and tamarack turning yellow. A light breeze carries the scent of Roy's rolled cigarette and the mix of horse shit, the smell of the forest, and other things I can't identify but imagine are the musk of deer, bear, and other wild creatures.

That evening, we follow a trail that switchbacks down a hillside into Berg Lake. A huge glacier perches on the mountain overhanging the cobalt-blue lake, and chunks of ice the size of a house calve off with ear-splitting roars. They explode into the lake like bombs, causing two-foot-high waves to crash against the far shore. I've never seen anything like it.

Roy leads us to some old cabins on the edge of the lake where we dismount.

"You boys can sleep in that cabin. We'll cook and sleep in the lodge." Roy points to a larger cabin.

We haul our duffels to the log cabin and set our sleeping bags on metal cots.

After dinner we turn in, exhausted from a long ride. I lie in my bag, and while my mind drifts back to the excitement of packing up, the horses, the beauty of the trail, and the glorious lake, I hear Don rapping his knuckles on the floor.

"Hey, stop it. I can't sleep." I don't want to admit I'm too excited to sleep.

"I thought that was you," Don answers.

"What?" I ask.

"Stop kidding around."

"That's not you?"

"No. You?"

The sound stops and we fall silent, waiting for it to start again.

*Bam, bam, bam, bam.* The staccato knocking begins anew.

"Think it's a griz?" I whisper. I don't want to add, "trying to get in to eat us?"

"Don't know," Don whispers.

The noise stops. I hold my breath.

The rapping begins again, then stops. I feel for my flashlight, wait for the knocking to start, then spot the villain. It keeps us awake all night.

The next morning at breakfast I tell Roy.

"Pack rat. Shoulda shot it," Roy replies.

"Next time." I don't want to sound stupid, so I don't ask what a 180-grain 30–06 bullet would do to the floor of the cabin.

Later that day, we climb a steep trail toward a mountain pass above tree line. We top the last ridge into the grassy depression and startle bedded bighorn rams. I count nine. They rise and trot fifty yards above us, then stop to look at us. Their full-curl horns are massive and their ends are broomed off fist-sized.

"Shoot! Shoot!" Roy wheels his horse and points at the rams. Don and I sit on our horses and watch the sheep watch us.

"Goddammit, get off your horse and shoot one!" Roy's horse spins around again.

"We came to hunt grizzlies, not shoot a damned sheep!" Now I'm swearing. Hell, when I was a kid on the farm I tended a herd of my father's sheep. Thirty-two of the stupidest animals God ever created. Open a gate for them and they'd crash into the barbed wire fence three feet away, get all cut up, and screw up the better part of a perfectly good August day at the swimming hole. I'd have to spend the afternoon catching them and painting their cuts with purple medicine. I don't want to shoot a damned stupid sheep!

"They're record-book rams!" Roy's face is livid.

I wonder what the "record book" is, as the bighorns trot up-hill and disappear over the ridge.

"You boys blew a lifetime opportunity!" Seething with anger, Roy throws down his cigarette butt, spurs his horse, and heads the packstring down the trail.

"We're hunting grizzlies," I mutter to Don.

"Yeah, nobody shoots sheep," he replies in a soft voice Roy can't hear.

I watch puffy white clouds gather into a solid mass that turns dark and starts to sprinkle cold drops of rain. The drops soon turn into a sheet of rain driven by a hard westerly wind. It turns to sleet, then wet snow by the time we arrive at Camp Creek to look for the lost stove, which remains lost, infuriating Roy even more.

I pull up the collar of my soggy wool coat and wonder how warm my cotton sleeping bag will be tonight. I was chilly last

night. The bag had been an eighth-grade Christmas gift pur-
chased from Sears, and now, six years later, I'm getting to use it
for the first time.

That night we make camp in the shelter of some trees near the
head of a valley. We set up wall tents and kick the snow from the
ground inside, spread a canvas horsepack cover as a ground
cloth, and toss my cotton sleeping bag on top. It looks pathetic. I
know it won't keep me warm. Don borrowed his uncle's bag, a
World War Two mummy bag. I'm envious.

At dinner in the warm cook tent, where Roy and his daughter
and son-in-law sleep, I wait until Roy steps outside, then ask if
there are any extra blankets.

"Naw, we're using the horse blankets for mattresses," son-in-
law says.

"Hot rocks," daughter says.

"Huh?" I can't believe what I'm hearing.

"Best thing to do is to get a couple of big rocks and put them
on the wood stove to heat up, then roll them to the bottom of
your bag when you hit the sack," daughter ventures.

Gives the term "hot rocks" new meaning.

It turns out to be a great idea—at first. When I roll the hot
rocks into the bag and climb in, the rocks burn my feet, then feel
good for about an hour, but turn ice-cold for the rest of the night.

Teeth chattering, I wonder how nice it would be to sleep in
the cook tent with daughter and son-in-law. I imagine Roy sleeping with his back to the warm camp stove. I hear the stove's
squeaky metal door open and the sound of wood being laid on
top of the hot embers and know it will be repeated throughout
the night.

In between the opening and closing of the stove door, I listen
to Don's soft snoring and the snow pelting the canvas tent. I
think this hunting deal might not be as neat as it sounds.

Then, carried on the wind from far above our tree-sheltered camp, comes the howl of wolves. I've never heard wolves howl before, but there were a lot of coyotes on the farm, and I know the sound of coyotes. These howls sure aren't coyotes. I shiver and my hand snakes out of my sleeping bag to touch the cold, reassuring steel of my rifle.

It's still pitch black when I hear the clank of a frying pan and coffee pot against the camp stove. A few minutes later, I smell sizzling bacon and bubbling hot coffee. I'm finished with being cold and get dressed.

"What're you doing up? They haven't called us yet." Don's voice is husky with sleep, and he rolls over and pulls the top of his mummy bag over his head.

"I'm ready to hunt griz." I don't want him to know that I wish I were home where it is warm.

I force my feet into frozen leather boots and decide that the next time I go hunting, if there will be a next time, I'll buy the best sleeping bag and boots I can afford.

After a breakfast of pancakes and bacon, we mount up. The starless sky is still dark, but not as black as when I walked over to the cook tent. Only an occasional flake of snow falls.

"You take Don down valley and look for bear tracks," Roy orders son-in-law.

"Where are we going?" I ask.

Roy's black eyes reflect the shaft of yellow light thrown from the gas lantern in the cook tent. He sweeps his arm through the dark in a 180-degree arc. "Up there."

That afternoon, on a snow-blown ridge high above timberline, Roy spots a mountain caribou. "It's a good bull, and we'll have a gut pile that'll draw a griz."

We spend an hour stalking the caribou and my excitement builds each minute.

"Now! Shoot!" he commands.

I drop to a kneeling shooting position. My rifle shakes so much that I'm going to miss the caribou. Then I imagine what Roy would do if I screw up; I concentrate and drop the bull with one shot.

"Congratulations," Roy says.

I think I see a flicker of a smile.

A few minutes later I hold the white-maned bull's antlers as Roy takes my picture. For the second time, my excitement fades into sorrow for killing such a magnificent creature.

That night I eat my first caribou meat. "Man, this is the best meat I've ever tasted!"

"You wouldn't say that if you'd shot one of those rams. Bighorns taste better than caribou." Roy looks at me through the flare of his match as he lights a cigarette.

"Still, it's the best I've ever eaten," I say, not wanting him to win every point.

After dinner, Don retires to his warm mummy bag, and dreading the prospect of another freezing night, I sit on a stump next to the warm stove.

"It's late. We got to get up early to hunt. Why don't you go to bed?" Roy asks me.

"Yeah, I'd better turn in." I'd like to switch places with him.

For the remainder of the week, we hunt up and down the mountains, through forested valleys, and on top of snow-blown ridges. We look at the gut pile several times each day, but there are no tracks around it. A giant grizzly should be easy to see against the snow, but we don't spot a bear. We do see tracks in the area, but it is as if these huge creatures are unwilling to sacrifice their lives to unworthy hunters.

Defeated, we pack up and trudge several days through the snow back to the ranch, then wave good-bye to son-in-law from the window of the eastbound train we'd flagged down.

Don and I settle into facing seats. I put my boots on top of the heat panel and wonder if my feet will ever feel warm again.

The train lurches forward, and Don leans toward the window to watch son-in-law drive the ancient truck back down the path toward Hargreaves' ranch.

"Wonder why old Roy didn't drive us?"

"Guess he was busy with something at the ranch," I say.

"Yeah." He leans back in his seat.

"Well, Don, what do you think about big game hunting?"

"It's okay." Don's eyes tell me that I'll never talk him into another hunt.

"What about you?" Don asks.

"I learned a lot." I'm not certain I'll ever go big game hunting again but don't want to admit that out loud. Might sound wimpy.

Still, I think as I look out the train window, there's something about the rugged snowcapped mountains, the glaciers, and yellow tamarack silhouetted against a crystalline blue sky that made a deep impression.

Maybe it's the smell of horses, or sizzling bacon, or pines.

Or the howling of wolves carried on the wind.

Or the sound of tumbling streams.

Or mountain sheep who scrunch their necks to carry their massive horns . . .

Maybe that's a part of it, and a big part of it, but not all of it. I can get all that by simply visiting the mountains in better weather.

The big thing is the anticipation that just over the next ridge there's a wild creature of power and dignity, courage and cunning. It's not the kill, I decide, it's the hunt.

It's during my time with Roy Hargreaves, a man as hard as his granite mountains, that the seeds of the hunt are planted in my soul. Seeds that will grow into a siren's call, enticing me to return, return.

# THE MOUTH

Bruce Creyke, the head guide for our hunting expedition, and I stand on the shore of Mowdade Lake in British Columbia watching the floatplane that flew us up the Stikine River from Wrangell, Alaska lift off and disappear over the trees on the far shore. It carries Jerry Mason and his partner, Dave George, who have just finished their hunting trip. Jerry's an interesting guy and I make a mental note to keep in touch.

My hunting partner, Doc England, is in the canvas wall tent, pulling on his waders. He intends to catch rainbow trout for dinner.

I look at Bruce. He's young, slender, five-foot-nine, and clothed in a Levi jacket with jeans tucked into cheap green rubber boots. Long black hair hangs below his black cowboy hat. A ragged scar slices across his cheek, and I know better than to ask.

He's rawhide tough. Standing next to him, I feel like the Pillsbury Doughboy dressed in the latest in outdoor fashions from Eddie Bauer.

"You set up this hunt. Who do you want for a guide?" Bruce asks.

I want to tell him that I live at low altitude in the Midwest, and that no matter how hard I'd tried to get into shape, he'd have me on my knees. I want to say "Please have patience, go easy, don't prove your manhood on me."

I'm shocked to hear my mouth say, "You can be my guide . . . if you're man enough."

Bruce stares at me, then nods. His lips are tight. The glint in his eye tells me he's accepted my mouth's challenge.

# TELEGRAPH CREEK

"There's a griz feeding on a kill." My guide, Bruce Creyke, is looking through his spotting scope at a flat of scrub willows far below.

"Where?" I ask, swinging my scope in that direction.

"See that point of spruce that sticks out on the left-hand side?" Bruce steadies his scope when a gust of wind hits. Clouds scud past.

"Yeah," I say, holding my breath.

"He's about 400 yards to the left of the last tree." Bruce turns the knob on his scope for better focus.

"Wow!" I lock on the grizzly bear, who is ripping meat off a dead moose. His silver-tipped hair waves in the wind like Nebraska wheat. I watch the bear turn the carcass over, then tear off another chunk. My muscles tighten.

An hour later, Bruce leads me down a game path toward the bear. I tug down the brim of my hat against the wind. The willows are taller than they looked from the mountainside. We can't spot the bear. It's spooky, knowing that a giant bear is hidden so near.

"Put a cartridge in the chamber of your rifle and put it on safe. We're close." Bruce waits for gusts of wind to cover the sound of our movement.

I chamber a round in my Winchester .264 Magnum, flip on the safety, and hold the barrel skyward. We inch forward, scanning every bush for the bear, for parts of the bear—an ear, eye, wind-ruffed hair—anything to see him before he spots us. Grizzlies defend their kills.

Bruce stops, holds up his hand, then points back the way we came. We retreat several hundred yards. "I don't like it. I can't see him."

I'm disappointed. It's been nine years since my first bear hunt with Don Trieschmann and Roy Hargreaves.

"He won't run from his kill," Bruce says, watching the brush.

"I know," I say.

"I'm going to climb that tree. Wait here, I'll see if I can spot him." Bruce walks toward a tree on the edge of the scrub willows several hundred yards away.

I remember a story about a wounded bear doubling back on his trail to ambush and kill his pursuer. How far will a griz go from his kill to protect it? I scan the bushes behind me.

I see Bruce, wearing his black cowboy hat, near the top of the tree, but I don't watch him long. I'm more interested in what might be creeping up behind me.

"See him?" I whisper when he returns.

"No. The brush is too high, but I spotted another game trail that leads that way. We'll use it. Be ready."

My muscles must be quivering from the cold wind.

We sneak down another trail that weaves through knee-high to shoulder-high willows, moving only when the wind blows. There's nothing. Nothing to see or smell. The wind slaps the willows against each other and their rustling smothers all other noise. I know the darned bear moved out and feel nauseous with disappointment.

*Woof!* Thirty yards ahead the griz rises above the brush on its hind legs and focuses on us. I snap off the rifle's safety. Bruce dives out of the way.

*Woof!* His paws hang in front of his chest. The tips of his curved claws are white.

I pull the rifle toward my shoulder, but my finger squeezes the trigger before I spot the bear in the scope. The bullet flies five feet over the bear's head.

The griz drops to all fours. I jack another round into the rifle's chamber. He runs at us, filling my scope. I pull the trigger. He screams, rolls, and tears willow bushes out a few yards in front of us. A shoulder shot.

Another shot. He bellows and a torn bush flies into the air. Then my last shot. The bear moans, quivers, and falls quiet. Is he dead, or is he gathering energy to charge? I reload and point the rifle at him. He doesn't move. My leg begins to dance and shake in a way that I hope Bruce doesn't see.

We skin him out, cutting out a backstrap so I can have a grizzly steak for dinner.

"Why couldn't we see him, Bruce?"

We find the spot where the griz stood up.

"He was sleeping on top of his kill," Bruce says. A half-eaten moose lies in a depression in the willows.

We gather our horses, wrap the meat and skull inside the bear skin, and lash it to Bruce's saddle.

He looks at the low hanging clouds. "Going to snow."

I nod and mount my horse, reining it behind his on the narrow trail that snakes through the wilderness. Bruce walks, leading his horse into a wind-driven white blizzard. Within minutes heavy white flakes turn him into a ghost that drifts in and out of sight. I tuck my chin into the collar of my coat, pull my hat low, urge my horse close to his, and think about the warmth of the wood stove waiting at camp. It would be a miserable night to sleep out.

We find our camp pitched next to a creek at the head of a narrow valley in the shelter of a spruce forest.

"Great bear! Congratulations." Doc England, my hunting partner, slaps me on the shoulder and hands me a cup of hot tea. I brush the snow off my hat and coat and duck into the warmth of the cook tent, where we eat dinner and tell stories about our day's hunt.

"I didn't spot anything, but my guide told me there are a lot of mountain caribou in the area. Maybe I'll find them tomorrow," Doc says.

The next morning, Doc lights the gas lantern hanging from our tent pole. When we walk through the dark toward the cook tent for breakfast heavy snow flakes float through the yellow lantern light. The world is white.

The cook tent is warmed by the wood stove. Doc pours a cup of coffee and asks, "What's that howling sound?"

"The wind blowing across the tundra up above," Bruce says.

"Oh." Doc picks up a piece of toast and slathers it with strawberry jam.

"We have to flesh out John's bear hide today, but if you'd like to hunt . . . ?" Bruce asks Doc.

Tommy, Doc's guide, buries his face in a metal mug of black coffee. It looks like he's praying.

"If I don't go out today, what are my chances for a caribou?" Doc asks.

"We leave for base camp tomorrow. It's the end of the hunt. Maybe we'll see one on the way back." Bruce glances at Tommy.

"Well, we might as well try today," Doc says.

Tommy looks crestfallen, but says nothing and leaves to saddle two horses.

I watch them mount up and wave good-bye as they turn their horses toward the gloom and disappear into the wall of snow.

I'm thankful I'm staying in camp to help Bruce tend to the trophies I've taken on this trip; a Stone sheep that'll go high in the record book, two mountain goats, and the griz. It's been a heck of a hunt, and I'm not anxious to fight wind-driven snow to look for caribou.

Bruce builds a fire near a spruce with overhanging branches. He cuts a six-foot-long green limb the diameter of my wrist, sharpens it with an ax, and drives it into the ground at an angle pointing to the fire. He disappears, then returns with the ribs of my sheep and impales them on the end of the stick.

"You'll like sheep ribs," Bruce says, sitting next to me. He picks up the bear skin, spreads it, hair side down, over our laps and pulls out his knife.

"Show me how to flesh it out," I say, unsheathing my knife.

"You never fleshed out a skin?"

We sit under the sheltering branches of the spruce and watch heavy snowflakes spiral down. Warmed by the bear skin, we listen to roasting sheep ribs sizzle and shave off small pieces of fat that could rot the skin. We toss the fat into the fire and listen to them hiss and sputter in the flames.

"Strong wind." Bruce tips his head toward the howling sound above.

"Think Doc'll get a caribou today?"

"Snow is blowing so hard they'll be lucky to see their horses' heads," Bruce says.

"I'm glad I'm not up there with them."

"Me, too."

I'm surprised he'd admit that, for he's young and strong.

He gets up, tosses three more sticks of wood on the fire, then cuts off several ribs. We sit under our shelter, bear skin over our laps, gnawing warm meat off bones.

# ALONE

"Goot ram! Ya, goot ram," the German hunter says over and over when he sees the Dall sheep horns lashed to my backpack. I lower my backpack to the ground and the man hobbles over, leaning on his walking stick, and runs his fingers over the horn, counting the ridges to determine the ram's age.

"Nine and a half," I say. It's a good ram, forty-two inches, but just misses the record book.

"Ya. Goot ram." He limps back and lowers himself to sit on a log in front of the tent. His right ankle is wrapped in an elastic bandage.

"Hurt yourself?" I ask.

The German shrugs his shoulders.

"He doesn't speak English," his guide says, stepping out of the tent. He sips on a coffee mug.

"What happened?"

31

"He wore boots with hobnails. Slipped on the rocks. Shouldn't ever wear hobnails," his guide says.

"I guess they'd be okay for stepping on wet logs and stuff," I say.

"Yeah, but how many wet logs do you find around here?"

"Not many."

"Take a look at his walking stick. It breaks down for travel. Looks rough, but it's pretty well made," his guide says.

The German hunter hands it to me when he sees me looking at it. Its wooden shaft is rough in my hand, and there's a steel screw-in adapter that holds the two pieces together. A four-inch steel spike protrudes from the end.

"It looks sturdy, but I'd hate to have to lug it around these mountains. And what's he going to do with this point, defend himself from a bear?" I stab the air.

The guides laugh, and the German looks perplexed. I hope he really doesn't understand English.

That night the guides decide the German shouldn't go home empty-handed. The plane won't be back to pick us up for three days. They'll go after a ram for him if I stay to look after him.

"Is that legal?" I ask.

"To look after him?" my guide asks.

"No, for you guys to shoot his ram," I say.

"I have a license. It'll be my ram. I'll give it to him as a gift. Besides, he'll appreciate it and give me a big tip," his guide says.

Using sign language, they explain to the German hunter what they are going to do. He frowns, then nods his head and says "Ya, ya."

I can't tell if he understands what the guides are going to do; if he knows it's illegal. I can't respect a hunter who breaks not only the law but the unwritten moral code of the hunt. The language barrier prevents me from talking to him about it. I feel depressed.

I cook for him while the guides are away. One afternoon he shows me his rifle. It's a single shot, with gold engravings of a boar and stags. The action fits tighter than any rifle I've held. It's a masterpiece of craftsmanship.

The scope is twist removable, but there's no question in my mind that it never loses its zero. The rifle is well-balanced and is the most beautiful weapon I've held to my shoulder. I'm envious, yet because of the language barrier I can't make him understand how much I admire it.

We try to converse as we eat. The loneliness of this wilderness mountain valley is heightened by our inability to talk about our families, jobs, lives, or to share hunting and fishing stories.

The German tries to tell me things. But what? Is he telling me he's getting sick? Loves my cooking? Hates it?

I try to communicate, draw pictures, try sign language. It doesn't do much good. My voice rises with frustration, as if he will be able to understand if I talk louder.

We must have a lot in common, like our love for hunting, but there's no way to share our experiences. We're like two deaf men grinding through each day until the end.

I feel more isolated than if I were alone. I imagine he feels the same way, because he becomes withdrawn and melancholy.

I've traveled to foreign countries where I didn't speak the language, but there were things to do, places to go, and when desperate I could always find someone who spoke English.

Isolated with this uncommunicative stranger inside a soggy tent in a narrow, rocky valley under leaden skies becomes a gloomy burden that weighs heavy on my soul. I've never felt so alone.

To escape, I take long walks. One day, after hearing howls from a pack of wolves, I try to call them in with a predator call. I think I sound like a gourmet meal, a dying rabbit, but they ignore me.

On the third day, the guides return with a small ram.

"Goot! Goot!" The German hunter is delighted.

When the plane lands on the gravel bar of the stream next to the tent, he motions me over and hands me his walking stick.

"Danka. Danka," he repeats over and over, bringing his hand to his mouth like he's eating my cooking.

I'm not about to take a tip for cooking and taking care of him for a couple of days. Besides, what would I do with the darned thing? I shake my head and smile and hand the stick back to him. He looks insulted and shoves it back.

"Danka!" The edge to his voice reveals his frustration. He thinks I don't understand his gesture of generosity. He hands it to me and at that moment I understand his desperate need to communicate his thanks.

I smile and take the walking stick and stroke it and nod and say "Danka" several times and wish we could have enriched each other's life with the simple gift of talking.

# CRASH LANDING

An arctic gust off the Bering Sea slams the right wingtip of the Piper Super Cub within inches of the river. We're going to crash.

Bush pilot Jack Lee jams the rudder to the left and hits a hard left aileron. Packed shoulder-tight into the back seat, I watch over Jack's shoulder as the alder and river rock-strewn peninsula rushes to fill the front windshield. The Super Cub's right wing inches up, but late. We're too low. I hold my breath and brace against the metal frame of the fuselage.

I think about Tish and my three little kids at home and realize how stupid I was to put them at risk. I vow that if I survive I'll never do it again.

The impact throws the plane over the two-foot-high river bank onto the gravel. G-force slams my body against the door. The plane skids and spins, tail first, to the left. As we ground-loop, my head bangs against the door frame. I lose count of the number of times we spin before a thick patch of alder bushes stop us.

In the silence, I marvel that Jack was able to cut the throttle and kill the engine so we won't have a fire. I hear my own gasping breath. I count my gasps, but I can't hear Jack's breathing.

"You okay?" I ask.

"Son-of-a-bitch!" Jack's fist hits the top of the instrument panel. Knowing he isn't dead floods me with a sense of relief. At least I won't die alone on the barren Alaskan Peninsula.

My body leans against the door. The little single-engine plane tilts at a crazy angle, its right wingtip rests on the gravel. My heart sinks when I spot branches of an alder bush poking through the wing's fabric. I know enough about aerodynamics to know a wing needs a solid, smooth surface for lift. Our wing is riddled with holes.

"May Day! May Day!" Jack screams into the microphone. He releases its key and waits for a response. We listen. Nothing. After ten minutes of calling May Days, Jack cradles the microphone.

Neither of us says the obvious, but I begin to feel alone.

"Might as well look at the damage," Jack says while he tries to pry the door open. It finally gives, snapping open under the wing. He crawls out.

I tumble out, fall on the ground, scramble up, and reach back into the cockpit to retrieve my .338 Winchester Magnum. This country is loaded with huge brown bears.

When we inspect the damage, we find the right landing gear is bent up at a fifty-degree angle. Its balloon tundra tire is still inflated but hangs a foot off the ground. Other than the fabric of the right wing and the tail being punctured and torn by alder branches, the body looks okay structurally.

I run my fingers along the edges of the prop. There are the normal nicks that bush props endure, but it's not bent.

"Prop looks okay," I say.

More alder branches poke through the fabric of the tail and rudder.

"Not too bad," Jack shakes his head.

"Uh-huh," I say. Bullshit, I think. I wonder how far a walk it would be to reach the coastline. A lot of bush pilots follow the coast. Then I remember that a downed pilot should stay with the plane because it's easier for rescuers to find. And, a cynical little voice whispers in my head, easier to identify your body.

Shaking off the voice, I walk twenty yards away to the edge of the river bank and unzip. The hood on my goose-down parka bangs up and down against my shoulder, making me realize that a strong wind is blowing. I turn downwind.

The sky is overcast, but it has been that way since I arrived at Ken Oldham's outfitting camp on Cinder River four days ago. It's early spring, and there is heavy snow remaining in the alder shadows and in the ravines.

When I turn back and look at our wreck, I realize we're lucky. We have matches. We can build a fire. There's one survival sleeping bag tucked in the back of the plane. We can sit out storms in the dry cockpit. I can shoot something to eat . . . if we see anything.

My most vivid impression from the past four days is the vast amount of country it takes to support one animal. There's plenty of water to drink. It might take a day or two for the outfitter to find us. We might get hungry, but we'll survive.

Jack reaches into the back of the Super Cub and pulls out a short-handled ax, rope, and a roll of tape. "You cut off whatever branches you can with your knife without tearing the fabric. I'm going to cut some alders."

He returns a short while later with three wrist-sized alders. "Lift the tip of the wing as high as you can while I hammer out this landing gear," he says.

He uses the back of the ax to straighten the aluminum gear, as I keep it off the ground by holding the wingtip over my head. I'm amazed this fragile craft can hold us up in flight. Each time Jack hits the landing gear, I'm certain it'll break in two.

When Jack gets the wheel pointed the right direction and close to the ground, he splints the dented and slightly bent landing gear with the thick alders and rope.

"Okay, John, you can lower the wing now," he says. "Easy!"

He didn't have to add "easy." I know the damned gear will collapse the minute I lower it to the ground. It holds.

Two hours later, we pull the plane from the alder branches and patch the holes in the fabric with the tape. Tape that I'm certain will rip off, piece by piece, when Jack tries to fly the wreck to get help to extract me from this godforsaken place.

"May Day! May Day!" Jack tries the radio again. Nothing.

Outfitter Kenny Oldham and my hunting companion, Bill Niemi, are out of radio range. Bill shot a humongous brown bear early yesterday morning. Today, they flew over to the Pacific coast to spot caribou, moose, sea lions, and other wildlife. They're on the other side of Anakchak Mountain, which splits the peninsula. Its mass blocks our radio transmission . . . if the radio still works.

Jack flips it off. "No sense in wasting the battery. We'll try later."

"Later?" I ask.

"Yeah. Since we're here, we might as well go bear hunting," Jack says with a grin.

"Don't you think it might be better for you to fly back to camp to get help?" I'm not about to get back into that airplane.

"Naw. Ken and Bill won't be back until late this afternoon. I'd like them to be overhead when we take off." Jack reaches into the Super Cub and pulls out a frame backpack and his rifle.

Two things bother me about his statement: First, if Jack wants Ken to be flying overhead when "we" take off, it means that he isn't sure that "we'd" make it. He wants to have immediate help available. Second, I sure don't like the "we" bit. I mentally reaffirm that I'm not going to climb back in that wreck.

My desire to hunt bear is dampened by the uncertainty of our situation, but I look at my watch to see it's just ten-thirty in the morning. Jack isn't going to try to get help until Ken and Bill are back in the vicinity, so I have the choice of going with Jack or sitting by the Super Cub all day. I remind myself that I did come up here to hunt bear.

I follow Jack up a ridge where we use our binoculars to search for bear. We look at miles of spring-gray tundra interspersed with gullies full of stark black alders, all blanketed by an oppressive, dull cloud layer. There are no living creatures; no grizzlies, moose, or caribou. No fox, ground squirrels, or mice. No nothing.

Bleak . . . Cold . . . Alone . . . Forever . . . depressing words skip across my mind like stones across water, then sink into my soul.

I scan the tundra and wonder about my reluctance to share my feelings with this man whom I met for the first time in the cook tent at base camp four days ago. I wonder if, under his calm exterior, he feels the same fears. Does he have qualms about getting back into his Super Cub and jamming the throttle to the firewall for perhaps the last time? Would talking about our fears help, or push us over the edge?

Eyes glued to my 10x40 Leitz binoculars, I mentally run through a check list of my alternatives. The list is damned short. I decide that my only alternative is to stay in the moment and enjoy the process.

"Let's move." Jack stands up, shouldering his pack and rifle.

About a mile upriver, we glass from another high spot.

"What's that dark spot in the alders next to the river?" I ask.

"Where?"

"See that sand ribbon that splits the snow and alders? It's at the upper end, on the left-hand side, in the middle of that big patch of snow." I point, but Jack is looking through his binoculars.

"Got it," he says.

"I can't tell if it's a big rock or a bedded griz." I roll to my stomach and place my binoculars on the crown of my cowboy hat to steady my vision.

"It's a bear. A good one." Jack's voice carries excitement . . . more than I've heard from him.

"Let's go," I say, putting my hat on.

"Wait. Check your rifle. Put one in the chamber."

I slide a .275-grain Silvertip into the chamber, drive the bolt home, and put the Winchester .338 Magnum on safety. I'll have a total of four shots before reloading.

"We'll creep up that sand ribbon. It's downwind. If we're real quiet the bear won't hear us."

"Okay." I stand up and bring my rifle up to test for loose clothing that could snag the stock and prevent me from getting off a quick, clean shot.

"One more thing. If you don't hit him in the shoulder with your first shot, he'll charge. Once you start shooting, keep on shooting until you're out of ammo. They're tough to put down."

"Where are you going to be?" I ask. I don't know if I'm concerned for his safety or mine.

"Next to you, but don't count on me because that bear can move so fast I might not get a clear backup shot. Don't screw up."

Yeah. Uh-huh.

We creep up the ribbon of sand until we're about seventy yards from the bear. I raise my rifle, look through the scope, and see nothing but alder bushes. I'm not about to risk a shot that could be deflected.

"Gotta get closer," I tell Jack.

We move closer, thankful that the snow has melted from the sand spit. It makes for quiet footing. I can see the bear well at fifty yards, but there's no shot. A step at a time, I move closer. Jack follows. I can hear him breathing.

At thirty yards, I have a clear shot. I hold on the bruin's shoulder and squeeze the trigger. The bear's roar and the explosion of my first shot blend into a hellish sound. He spins, growling. I shoot again and again and again. The bear collapses on his back in the snow among broken alders.

I reload and watch the bear. It's still.

"You've got him," Jack says.

We plow our way through the alders to the bear. He lies on his back on the snow. His front paws are raised close to his shoulders as if to strike. I touch his eye with the barrel of my rifle. He doesn't blink.

Jack pumps my hand and slaps me on the back. I look at the lifeless bear and a wave of sadness dampens my feelings of happiness. I say a silent prayer of thanks to the bear's soul.

"Give me your camera and I'll take a picture," Jack says. He leans his rifle barrel in the fork of an alder branch.

Alders are so thick that I have to step over the bear to get on the other side for the picture. I swing my right leg up and over the bear's chest. His claws are inches from my crotch. I see his long canine fangs. My left foot crashes through the crust of the snow, and I fall onto the bear. He convulses. His front legs jerk and his claws fly toward my crotch.

I scream, jump, and fall off the far side of the bear. I lie silent in the snow, waiting for the bear to roll over and finish me off. My rifle has disappeared. Gasping for breath, I watch the bear next to me. He's still.

Jack's laughter registers in my consciousness, and I want to sink under the snow until I end up on some warm white sand beach far away from this situation.

Hours later, after skinning the bear, we cut out his tenderloins and cook one over a wood fire. With full bellies, we arrive back at the Super Cub. At least we won't be hungry if we crash and die on takeoff. Jack radios for Ken but gets no response.

"Maybe the radio isn't transmitting. We might as well try it," Jack says as he stuffs his rifle and pack in the back of the plane.

"Yeah. Well . . ."

"You wait here while I taxi down the gravel bar to be in position for takeoff. I don't want your extra weight until then. Once I'm there, bring the bear hide and pile in." Jack eases into the cockpit. The 150-horsepower Lycombing engine kicks to life, and he eases the plane down the gravel bar. I watch it bump over the rocks and wait for the landing gear to collapse. It doesn't.

I think about my alternatives. One is to refuse to go. I could wait here for Jack to send Ken back to pick me up with his plane. But what if Jack crashes on the way back? Rescuers might spot the wreckage, but there'd be no way in hell they would find me. And what if Ken and Bill had trouble? I might spend a couple of days alone in the bush without cover. While I don't want to admit it, watching the claws of that bear jerk toward my crotch has made me irrationally superstitious. If I stay, some other bear, seeking revenge, will chow down on *my* tenderloins.

I pile into the back seat and Jack dumps the bear skin on my lap. I take consolation in the fact that I'm firmly jammed in. If we crash again, I'll be cushioned, and my life perhaps saved by the hide of the bear I've just killed. I can't find humor in the irony.

Jack keeps the brakes on while the engine revs to full throttle. The vibration of the plane covers my shaking. He releases the brakes and the Super Cub bounces like a gooney bird down the gravel bar, gathering speed until the tail wheel lifts off. Now maximum weight is thrust on the damaged landing gear. This is when it will collapse.

Jack's left hand jerks up on a handle and the flaps ram full-down. The little plane hops off the gravel bar, shudders, then gains altitude, slowly.

I sigh. We've made the first part of our journey home. The spot where we will land at base camp is smooth sand. We should be all right . . . unless the tape on the wing and tail tears off. I watch a loose piece flap against the wing and pray it sticks.

I can't see the tape on the tail, but my imagination senses it tearing, inch by inch, peeling away from the fabric. My back feels the vibrations that will increase until the tail fabric rips off and we spin to our death.

The tape holds.

We circle the tents at base camp twice before Jack can spot the smoke from the cook stove which indicates the direction to land. I brace myself when he turns for a short final approach. Using full flaps, the Super Club flares just a foot above the sand beach until it reaches stall speed. He inches in power to prevent stalling and dips the left wing to touch down on the Super Cub's good left gear. Airspeed falling, the plane gently settles on the crumpled right gear. Tilted to the right, we taxi into camp.

Jack uses the powerful base camp radio to order replacement parts. Another pilot will ferry the parts down the coast tomorrow, next day at the latest. Jack will have the plane in shape before his next clients arrive.

I'll be happy when I get my feet on home ground.

Author's note: *It is interesting to note how the concepts of hunting ethics change over time. For example, using bush planes to spot game on the same day as the hunt was legal and considered ethical in Alaska during the late 1950s and early 1960s, when the events in this story occurred. At that time, flying was more dangerous than hunting bears. There wasn't much hunting pressure. However, as more and more hunters experienced the same-day hunt by air, many sportsmen began to question the ethical aspects of using hi-tech transportation to reach big game animals. Famed outdoor editor and big game hunter Jack O'Connor was one of the first to question the ethics of the practice through his columns in* Outdoor Life. *Hunters, conservationists, and state game officials soon started the movement that led to the banning of same-day hunting by air.*

# HOW YA GONNA
# MOUNT IT?

Ken Oldham and Bill Niemi land in Ken's Piper Super Cub at our Cinder River bear hunting camp at dusk, with word that a storm out of Siberia is blowing across the Bering Sea toward us. We decide we'd better pull out in the morning. We contact a pilot who is ferrying a hunter out of a camp at Port Heiden and has room for two more passengers. We can get to King Salmon and on to Anchorage before the storm hits.

Alerted by a radio call from the pilot of a Cessna 180, we are waiting the next morning with our gear outside camp when he lands. An ebullient Texan jumps out and immediately collars Bill to tell him about his hunt. While the pilot and I load our duffels and rifles and my bear hide, I tell him that I fly a Bonanza G-35 and, being the heaviest, I should sit in the co-pilot's seat.

The other hunter sits behind the pilot, then Bill scrambles into the back seat next to him and the pilot and Ken Oldham push, jam, and cram Bill's immense bear skin onto his lap. I try not to laugh. Bill looks like a gnome peeking over the top of the pile on his lap.

The other hunter is continuing to regale Bill with his manly feats and raises his voice over the roar of the engine when we take off. I wave at Ken and Jack who stand next to the tents below.

Bill is a small, quiet man with a delightful, wry sense of humor. He told me that he'd won his company, Eddie Bauer, during a crap game at the end of the Second World War. By the 1960s, the company is a premiere outdoor clothing and equipment company and owes much of its success to Bill's constant testing of new products during hunting trips all over the world. He'd lost a finger to frostbite when he pulled his hunting partner from the Arctic Ocean during a polar bear hunt. He was a man who'd been there and done everything.

The Texan has Bill trapped, speechless, under his bear skin. " . . . and that damned bear charged me and I shot him and he fell so close that blood splattered over my guide's boots. That guide would have died if I wasn't such a good shot."

The pilot looks at me and raises his eyebrow. I grin and feel happy that I'm not sitting in back with the loudmouth. The heater warms the inside of the cockpit, and Bill's bear skin begins to stink. He's going to have bear grease all over the front of his pants.

" . . . got back to camp and measured that bear. It's going to be up in the top of the record book. I can't stop thinking how lucky my guide was that I'm such a great shot. If it had been anyone else . . ."

We fly a hundred feet off the ocean shore, and when the pilot banks to the right, I spot the reflection of Bill's face peering over the top of the bear skin. His eyes are glassy, and he stares straight ahead while the words of the other hunter engulf him.

An hour of bragging later, I can make out the runway at King Salmon in the distance. The cloud cover presses down on us, and the constant bragging of the hunter in the back seat grinds down my nerves. I notice the pilot's fingers inch the throttle in to increase the engine's rpm. Increased speed means we get on the ground and away from the loudmouth a few minutes faster. Enduring his BS makes every minute seem like an hour. I pity poor Bill. His left ear is inches from his tormentor's lips.

". . . and I'm going to get my bear mounted life-sized. Yes, sir! I'm going to put him in the corner of my office. It'll be a full mount . . . in charging position!" The hunter waits for a comment from Bill. Bill says nothing.

The runway looks closer now. I feel like rocking my butt to hurry the plane along. The so-called terminal at King Salmon is a small shack. I dread the thought of being stuck listening to this guy until the commercial plane comes to take us to Anchorage. I look at my watch. It'll be a six-hour wait with that guy. I wonder if I have any bullets for my rifle handy.

"Yes, sir! A full mount . . . in charging position. His claws will be up, like this . . . like he's ready to rip you to shreds. . . Boy, that'll be something!" He pauses again to get agreement from Bill. Nothing.

The runway is close now, and the pilot's face is locked with firm determination. I hope he has the patience to land the plane before he bails out, screaming.

Bill is still silent. I hope he hasn't had a heart attack, but I dare not look. The damned guy might start on me.

He starts on Bill again. "Yep, mounted in charging position. What'd ya think about that?"

Bill says nothing. Maybe he's been smothered by the bear skin on his lap.

"Uh . . . I see you got one," the loud mouth says to Bill.

"Yeah." Bill's voice is hollow and strong.

"How big?"

"Big enough." Bill's voice is sarcastic. I feel happy Bill has survived the trip.

"How ya gonna mount it?" the hunter asks.

"I'm going to mount it life-sized . . . in crapping position."

# REVENGE OF THE LION

"Ve got a mountain lion dat moved into our bighorn sheep winter range. He's slaughtering da rams. I can get you a hunting permit and a pack of hounds, but you got to come quick!" Heinz Luenberger's Swiss accent gets thicker when he is excited, especially on the phone.

"Is he big?" I glance at my calendar; I can move things around. I know the flight schedule to British Columbia by heart.

"Ya . . . big tracks anyway."

"I'll pack my longbow and be there tomorrow." Hunting a mountain lion with hounds didn't sound very sporting, but using a bow would turn it into an adventure.

"Maybe you vant to bring your rifle, instead." A note of uncertainty creeps into his voice. Heinz has never guided a bowhunter. I'd packed a 7mm Magnum Ruger Single Shot rifle when I shot my bighorn ram with him.

"Don't worry, Heinz, you can back me up."

"Vell . . ."

I cut him off before he can say no. I cancel plans, apologize to Tish, and by flying stand-by, get to Cranbrook that night, where Heinz picks me up.

The next day, Heinz's Jeep plows through ten inches of fresh snow that blanket the old logging road. Evergreen branches droop under the weight; the contrast between white and green is startling. High above us, on the right, the perpendicular crags of the Chinese Wall are bathed in the alpenglow of the sun that will soon burst over the horizon.

The two hounds sprawled in the back snore as the Jeep's four-wheel-drive geartrain grinds, shattering the early morning silence.

"I didn't know you had two hounds."

"Ya, vell da big one is mamma of my Missy. She belong to my friend, Fritz, over in Cranbrook. He treat Heidi like she is a member of da family. No way to treat damn dog."

Heinz fights the steering wheel as he punches through a drift, then digs under his jacket, fishes out a pack of cigarettes, flicks one between his lips, and returns the pack to his shirt pocket.

I suck in a deep breath of fresh air, knowing it will be my last until we get out of the Jeep. It's the only thing I don't like about Heinz, the continuous smoking and the hacking between smokes. He's going to kill himself, but that's his choice.

Without taking his eyes off the smooth ocean of snow ahead, his fingers search for a kitchen match in his coat pocket. He strikes one with his thumbnail and lights up. When he exhales, a cloud of smoke hits the inside of the windshield, is captured by the stream of air from the defroster, and dispersed. I hold my breath but know it's useless.

We plow through thick pine, spruce, and tamarack forests, wind-blown meadows, and along a partially frozen river in a pristine valley that is overhung by monolithic cliffs. We cut elk, deer, and bighorn sheep tracks, but no lion tracks. I wonder if the cat has moved on.

By noon the landscape no longer appears soft. The sun's glare is harsh and cold. We stop next to a spring, and Heinz opens the back to let the hounds out. Warm and comfortable, they don't move.

"Lazy dogs! Get out. Ve gonna pee!" Heinz grabs Missy's collar and yanks her into the snow. She looks at him with a baleful eye. Heidi grunts, struggles to rise, then flops out of the Jeep. She stands in the snow and looks like she'll fall asleep again. Hell, they're so lazy their tails don't even wag.

I'm not impressed with our "pack" of hounds.

"Ve have lunch. You build fire." Heinz reaches into the Jeep and pulls out his pack.

Hungry, with cheeks burning in the bitter cold, I snap off dead twigs and branches from a spruce tree and start a fire against a granite boulder. Heinz wades through snow to fill his Billy-pot with spring water. The pot is a big tin can with a wire handle. Cheap and practical. He returns, jams a long straight branch deep into the snow, and hangs the pot over the crackling fire. He reaches into his pack, tosses me a sandwich, and drops several tea bags into the Billy-pot.

I find a forked branch, lay my ham-and-cheese sandwich on it, and hold it directly in the flames.

Heinz squints from the smoke of the cigarette dangling from his mouth. "You gonna burn it."

"The hotter, the better." I grin and wait for him to look away before lifting my stick higher. The dogs smell the food and meander over. Even food doesn't cause their tails to wag.

Heinz and I stand close to the fire, watching the water in the pot, waiting for it to boil. I nod toward the dogs.

"Ever hunted cats with these?"

He pours the hot water into a plastic cup, hands it to me, then pours himself a cup. "Ya. With my friend Fritz, and Heidi, there. I ask Fritz to hunt with us, but he busy. Heidi's a good hunter. This is Missy's first time. That's why I ask Fritz if I can bring Heidi. Heidi will teach her. He loves that dog. Sure hope nothing happens to her."

"What could happen?" The tea is strong and hot.

"Sometimes a wounded mountain lion kill a dog. Maybe you should use my rifle."

"I'll stick with my bow." Nothing will happen to Heidi; these dogs are worthless. Maybe I made a mistake in rushing out here. A waste of time. At least the company's good, scenery spectacular, and the tea hot.

We put out the fire, lift the dogs into the Jeep, and start driving again. Warmed up, I'm dozing when Heinz shouts.

"There it is!" Bounding tracks cut across the lane. We jump out and kneel down to examine the huge paw prints.

"Dat's da one! Get your bow." Heinz rips open the back of the Jeep and shouts at the hounds, "Heidi, Missy! Out! Out! Lion!"

Missy raises her head and looks at Heinz. Heidi doesn't even open her eyes. I sling a quiver full of arrows over my shoulder, watch the dogs, and decide it's useless. Heinz drags one dog out of the Jeep then the other, urging them toward the lion's track. They're bored.

Missy squats to pee.

My confidence sinks to a new low.

Heinz drags Heidi through the snow until her head is over the track. Flaccid, she looks up at him, then stares longingly at the Jeep. Using both hands, Heinz pushes Heidi's nose into the track.

The first movement is the twitch of her nose, then I hear her sniff. Another twitch, a louder sniff. Her head buries deep into the lion's track and her ears flick back and forth. More sniffs. A quick movement of her nose to the left, then deeper into the snow. The muscles in her baggy neck begin to quiver. Wave-like, that quiver runs through her massive body until her limp tail snaps ramrod stiff. Her Jell-O-like body transforms into hard muscle. Heidi raises her head and issues a howl that starts deep inside her chest.

I shiver.

Heinz grins at me.

Missy bounces forward and she, too, changes from an armchair pet into a primitive beast.

Baying, they bounce from track to track, back and forth, trying to figure out the direction the lion headed. Something happens inside of me, too. It's an atavistic, muscle-tensing feeling that links me to prehistoric hunters.

Heinz nods and flips his cigarette into the snow. He slings his rifle over his shoulder. The hunt is on.

The hounds bound up the mountain on the lion's track. We follow. They are soon out of sight, but their deep voices slice the icy stillness.

Within a half hour, I'm sweating and gasping for air. I'm dropping behind Heinz and resent it. He's five-foot-five and can't weigh over one-hundred-thirty pounds; I'm six feet and weigh two-hundred-ten. I'm twenty years younger. He lives at this altitude; I live three thousand feet lower. But still, he smokes three to four packs of cigarettes a day; his lungs must be screaming, he's got to stop. He continues to pull away. Embarrassed, I call out to ask him to wait.

When I catch up, he says, "Listen!"

The voices of the hounds are more excited, their bays shorter, almost barks.

"They got lion treed. Ve go!"

We follow their track to the top of the ridge, then stop and listen. Their voices change again, back to the original bays.

"Damned cat jumped out of the tree. He's moving again."

Panting, we listen to their voices fade, then five minutes later, we hear them again.

"Come on, they're going up there." Heinz points to the opposite hillside. We can't see them because of the trees. So we plunge, slip and slide down this side of the valley and scramble up the other side.

"Treed," Heinz shouts.

The change in their voices propels my feet. I notice the sun has gone over the mountain. We don't have much more daylight. I push out of my mind the thought of not catching up with the lion before dark.

Halfway up to the ridge where the lion was treed, the hounds' voices change.

"Damn cat jumped out of tree!" Heinz stops. We wait to see which way the lion will lead the dogs this time.

"Maybe we can cut a corner," I wheeze and worry about the approaching dusk. I feel sweat freeze to my neck hair.

Following the baying of the hounds, we retrace our steps, hit the valley floor, and once again climb up the other side.

"Got him treed again."

The hounds sound close when we top the ridge.

I spot their tracks and point. "There!"

We follow three sets of tracks along the ridgeline, then see movement a hundred yards below us. The two hounds are jumping at the base of a huge evergreen. When we get close, I can make out the lion crouched on a large limb about thirty feet high.

He is immense. I notch an arrow and move into position for a shot.

"Hit him in the chest—low in the chest! Kill him dead. Don't want a wounded dog!" Heinz stands next to me.

The hateful yellow eyes of the lion watch me. I calculate the distance. Is he calculating, too? I feel an adrenaline surge.

I raise my longbow, pick a hair on the lion's chest just above the limb, and loosen my arrow. My shaft flies swift, its razor-sharp broadhead strikes an inch or two low . . . into the tree limb.

The lion's fangs snap my wooden shaft in half, and he spits it back at me.

"Again! Again! Before he jumps," Heinz shouts.

Just as the lion jumps toward the trunk of the tree, my second shaft plunges into his chest. He climbs higher, then loses his grip and starts a slow slide down. I hear his claws rake bark from the tree. In the dusk, I can barely make out the fluorescent fletching of my arrow against his chest.

"The dogs!" Heinz rushes under the tree in an attempt to pull the dogs to safety. One slash of a lion's claws will eviscerate a hound. Heinz grabs their collars and drags them back.

I nock another arrow, but don't have time to shoot. The dying lion uses the last of his desperate strength to hold onto the trunk of the evergreen, yet the weight of his body drags him down.

He falls on the far side of the tree and slides down the snowy slope.

Heidi tears out of Heinz's grasp and rushes after the lion. "Damn! Heidi, come back!" Helpless, we watch the lion and Heidi drop out of sight.

I follow the saucer-like tracks. It's steeper than it looks. My feet slide, and for the first time, I can make out the edge of a cliff. I'm sliding toward the edge, faster, out of control.

Panicked, I use both hands to jab my longbow into the snow to arrest my slide. I stop several feet short of the face of the cliff. A hundred feet below I see the inert jumbled bodies of the lion and Heidi.

A half hour later, as a full moon casts silver shafts between tree shadows, we reach them. Steam rises from their bodies. The lion is still. Heidi's chest heaves with shallow breaths. Heinz touches the lion's eye with the muzzle of his rifle.

"Dead."

The lion and Heidi fell onto a heap of rocks at the base of the cliff, then slid thirty feet through the snow to rest side by side.

"Oh, shit," Heinz mumbles over and over. His worst fear has come true. His friend's dog is hurt. How bad? Maybe the fall just knocked her breath out. We crouch over Heidi. Talk to her. She barely lifts her head.

I run my fingers over her neck and chest, feeling for blood or broken bones. She doesn't respond. I feel her chest between her front legs, then slide my fingers downward until I feel a large soft bulge near her belly. It looks as though her insides have split through their lining. She barely moves her head at my touch.

I look up at Heinz. "She's hurt bad. We've got to get her out of here."

Heinz shakes his head. "Can't drag her. Maybe make a litter. We can leave the lion."

I can tell he's thinking about his friend Fritz. What's Heinz going to tell him: "Sorry, we killed your best friend"?

"Don't have time, Heinz. I'll carry her."

"She heavy," he says.

"Yeah. Help me get her up on my shoulders." I lay my quiver next to the lion and unstring my bow. I'll use it as a walking stick, for balance.

"She might bite your ear off."

"Don't think so. She's in shock. It's our only chance."

I brace for her teeth when we lift Heidi over my shoulders in a fireman's carry. She moans, and I can't tell if she knows friend from foe. At least she doesn't bite me. After thirty yards, I stick my bow in the snow and leave it. I need both hands to balance Heidi.

Several hours later, Heinz drops me off at his cabin. It's on the way to the vet; I'm exhausted, and I suspect he doesn't want me with him when he tells his friend, Fritz.

The next morning, over a late breakfast of fried eggs and bacon, Heinz tells me that Heidi suffered internal injuries. It might be touch and go, but the vet thinks she could make it.

"What about your friend?"

Heinz takes a long drag on his cigarette and exhales. "Fritz understand. Risk of lion hunting."

"At least she's alive." I fold three crisp pieces of bacon into a piece of jellied toast.

"Fritz loves to elk hunt. He wants to take you elk hunting next fall."

"Huh?"

"I tell him how you carry his Heidi out of da woods. You saved her. He want to pay you back."

"That's nice. Does he know I shoot a bow?"

"He think it's stupid, but want to take you anyway."

We pull a wooden toboggan to haul the lion out of the woods. It's even colder than yesterday, well below zero. When we find him, he's frozen solid. It's nightfall before we get back to the cabins.

"Ve have to thaw him out. Put him in your cabin. Keep the wood stove going tonight and ve skin him in the morning." Heinz and I lift the board-like mountain lion into the tiny cabin I'm using. The inside is just large enough to hold a bed and a pot-bellied wood stove. The outhouse is twenty yards behind the cabin. The lion just fits between my bed and the stove. He's as long as the bed.

When I excuse myself from the dinner table to return to the cabin, Heinz says over his cigarette in the corner of his mouth, "Don't let that lion get you in the middle of the night."

"He's dead." I smile.

"I've hear frozen mountain lions sometimes come back to life. Be careful." His eyes twinkle.

I laugh and say good night. My cabin smells like wild animals. I stoke the stove with a couple more chunks of wood, step over the lion, and climb into my sleeping bag. In the reddish glow of the stove I study the animal. It's magnificent. I remember the way his eyes looked at me before I shot him. Then I remember stories of frozen humans returning to life when thawed. I try to drive stupid thoughts out of my head. My fingers trace the arrow wound on the lion's still-frozen chest. Fitful, I struggle for sleep.

In the middle of the night, still awake, I toss more wood in the stove and feel the lion's body. It's thawing.

Sleep finally blankets me. Sometime later, a noise jars my eyes open. I lie still, searching the outlines of the cabin in the soft glow of the wood stove. I try to sort out if it was my imagination or an actual sound that startled me awake. I look at the huge cat next to me, then touch his belly. His front leg twitches.

I spring to the top of my bed, standing naked on tiptoes. I watch the lion, look at the door, watch the lion, the door, the lion. The only sound in the cabin is the hissing of the fire and the gasping of my breath.

Embarrassed, I look around, overwhelmed with the irrational thought that Heinz is watching. I grin, lie down, and try to go back to sleep. Every time I drift off, the thawing body of the mountain lion farts, twitches, or jerks. I watch him all night long.

The next morning, I stagger over to the main cabin for breakfast. Heinz looks at me and says, "Godt, you look terrible. Vat wrong?"

When I tell him the story of the lion keeping me awake all night, he grins and says, "That lion, he get revenge."

# GETTING EVEN

The man who meets me at the door of Heinz Luenberger's cabin in the mountains of British Columbia has world-weary eyes set deep in a hatchet-faced, crew-cut skull. His black eyes bore into me, judging, measuring. I try not to blink.

A plaid shirt and forest-green wool pants above well-oiled leather boots cover his ramrod-straight body. He's clean and lean and hard.

I drop my backpack on the wooden porch, lean my longbow against the cabin wall, and stick out my hand to introduce myself.

"Fritz," he replies in a strong accent, using only his first name.

Must be Swiss, like Heinz, I think. On the other hand, I'm not sure. If the accent isn't Brooklyn, Chicago, or Dallas, I get a little lost.

I return his firm grip and feel his callused hand pump mine up and down with one quick motion. At the same time, his head dips in a curt nod. My imagination hears his heels click.

Heinz appears in the doorway next to Fritz. The corners of his eyes smile when he sees me, and the cigarette that droops from the corner of his mouth bobbles when he speaks. "You met Fritz. He own Heidi, the hound you save last winter. Fritz want to find you an elk."

Carol, Heinz's wife, invites us into the kitchen for a cup of tea. Taking the teapot off the top of the wood cook stove, she looks like Santa Claus's wife. Surrounded by the smell of something baking, we sit around a long table that is covered with a red-and-white-checkered, plastic tablecloth and get caught up on family news.

Fritz remains silent, watchful.

Suddenly, Carol heaves out of her chair, grabs a hot pad in each hand, and opens the oven door. I'm hit with a blast of hot scent that makes me salivate. Carol smiles as she presents me with a steaming apple pie. The sugar she'd sprinkled over the crust is golden brown. Perfect!

"Your favorite, John!"

"Any pie is John's favorite." Heinz laughs.

After I've finished my second piece and drained my cup of tea, Fritz interrupts our conversation.

"I vant to camp high tonight. Ve should get going."

I change into my camouflaged hunting clothes and toss my pack into Fritz's Jeep. He watches me carefully as I place my longbow and quiver of arrows carefully between our packs. I know he's thinking it's a puny weapon, and I'm happy he keeps silent.

Heinz wraps his arm around Carol's waist when they wave good-bye. As the Jeep turns out of the lane, I look back to watch them walk toward their log cabin which is tucked under a grove of towering pines that soften the harsh snow-capped peaks to the west. I notice Carol slip her arm around Heinz, too, and I imagine they'll spend the rest of the afternoon listening to the breeze caress the pines and making love.

Fritz drives south for several miles, then picks up an old logging road that meanders upward through the forest.

"So, where do you live, Fritz?" My opening gambit receives a one word answer, as do my next three attempts to engage him in conversation.

Unsmiling, he asks me no questions, so I join him in silence. Apparently he's a man who either enjoys his own company or is shy or highly introverted or . . . mad. I decide he's shy. Heinz wouldn't put me in the woods with a psycho. I hope.

Sometimes I talk too damned much, particularly when I'm trying to get to know someone. Someone I'm going to be living with for the next week or so. It won't hurt me to be quiet for a while. I give Fritz space.

We stop at the end of the logging road and put on our packs. I string my bow and drop in behind Fritz on a game trail that winds upward through thick stands of pine and tamarack.

The short carbine that Fritz carries is slung over his shoulder, muzzle down. I think that's an unusual way to carry a rifle; most hunters sling their rifles muzzle up.

His pace is measured and I have no trouble keeping up for the first half hour. Then the trail steepens and I fall behind. When I gasp for a rest, he stops, faces forward on the trail and waits for my breathing to calm. He doesn't waste energy talking. It doesn't look like he wastes any energy.

Two sweaty hours later, near treeline, we find a small, tree-studded meadow. A gurgling spring feeds a rivulet with cold, clear water. I rinse my face, drink, then fill my canteen.

There are animal beds in the grass. I point. Fritz nods and motions me over to a huge pile of grizzly bear scat. When he turns to set his pack down, I poke the dung pile with a finger-sized stick. It breaks through the thin outer crust into a soft, warm mass.

The bear must have bedded here last night. I try to remember how far bears travel in a day. He must be twenty miles away by now. Or is it wishful thinking?

There are four beds, but only one pile of scat. Maybe there aren't four bears, but only one that had a bad night. Maybe. Or a sow with three cubs.

Maybe they'll return after dark.

Fritz lashes a pole three feet high between two pines, sets the end of a tarp over it, then uses another log to pin the far end of the tarp to the ground. I toss my down sleeping bag next to his and notice we don't have much more daylight. I start to gather squaw-wood for a fire.

Fritz shakes his head. "No fire. Smoke will spook the elk."

Okay, I think, how're we gonna cook dinner?

I watch Fritz reach into his pack and dig out a long roll of sausage and a block of cheese. He motions me to sit next to him on a large log, and he cuts off a chunk of each. It's good. I wonder if it's an appetizer or dinner.

Fritz flicks a cigarette into the corner of his lips and lights up. I watch the glow of the cigarette highlight his rugged face. His eyes stare into the dusk while a thin stream of smoke curls into the night sky. I want to ask him if cigarette smoke will bother the elk, but he has the rifle and there are bears around and it will be pitch-black in ten minutes and I don't want to piss him off. Besides, I don't think he has much of a sense of humor.

I climb into my bag and watch the stars pop out like exploding popcorn. I see Fritz tuck his carbine next to his sleeping bag
and my mind wrestles with why the man is so silent. Later, a soft
breeze lulls me to sleep.

The next morning, in the dark, we climb to the top of the ridge
overlooking the next valley and conceal ourselves in some boulders. Fritz fishes an elk bugle out of his pack. In the leaden gray of
dawn, he gives a series of screams and grunts. There's no answer.

"Elk are always here. Something's wrong," Fritz says to himself. I sure as hell don't know. Maybe they smelled his cigarette.

When the rising sun drives the shadows from the narrow tree-
less valley below, we have our answer. Four hundred yards directly below us, four golden grizzlies munch on berries. The
largest sits on its haunches and uses its massive paws to gather
the bushes close to its chest. Through my binoculars, I watch it
delicately nibble each succulent berry.

Fritz touches my arm and points three hundred yards down
valley. Three black bears are busy eating berries. Both groups of
bears should see each other, and with the sun warming the air
currents the grizzlies should get the scent of the black bears, but
they ignore each other.

"I thought grizzlies kill black bears," I whisper, breaking my
vow of silence.

"Too much food." Fritz smiles.

It's the first crack in the granite wall of his face, and I feel the
thrill of a minor victory.

We watch the two groups of bears for the better part of an
hour, then slip back over the ridge to hunt another valley. It's
fruitless. I follow Fritz back to camp, where he builds a small
fire to boil tea water. We sit on the log, and he cuts off another
chunk of sausage and cheese.

"Bear, they bugger the elk. Ve'll move up the ridge to another basin. Maybe better." It's the longest speech Fritz has given.

I seize the opportunity. "I notice you carry your rifle military fashion. Were you in the army?"

"Ya."

"The Canadian army?"

"Da German army." He falls silent again.

"It must have been terrible."

"Vorse than that."

I wait, but there is to be no more. We break camp and hike four hours to another mountain drainage where we set up camp and hunt until dark without success.

Since there are no elk to spook, we build a small fire, eat sausage and cheese, then Fritz pulls out his cigarette. Only one a day . . . disciplined. He produces a second knife from his pack and starts sharpening it with the knife he carries on his belt.

"I've never seen that," I say.

"Vhat?" The evening stillness is cut by the sound of his rhythmic metallic strokes.

"Never seen anyone sharpen one knife against another."

"Vorks goot. Sharpening stone veighs the same as a knife. Two knives are better," he said.

"Learn that in the army?"

"Ya."

"I was too young for the Second World War. Tell me about it," I gamble.

Fritz puts his knives away, throws another piece of wood on the fire, and looks into the flames.

"Da depression. I vas hungry. No jobs. Money vas vorthless. You vere lucky to get money to buy sausage, prices doubled by the time you run to the market. No hope," he shakes his head. "Ve had no hope."

"It must have been awful."

"Ya. You hate Hitler. He did terrible things, but in the beginning he gave us jobs and food and hope for future.

"I lived in a small village in Austria. All da boys joined da youth movement. Ve had uniforms and pride."

Amazed at the words flooding out of Fritz, I slide off the log and use it as a back rest. I'd grown up hating the Nazis and Hitler and the Germans.

Fritz pokes the fire and sparks drift into the night sky. "Vhen da war breaks out I join the army. The SS, a paratrooper. I vas hero in my village. People cheered me, gave me food, lagers, girls kissed me . . .

"I parachuted into da edge of Moscow and fought behind the lines until I could get back. Ve had light summer uniforms. Winter set in.

"You know about German efficiency? Vell, it's a myth. Vhen da first supply train got through it contained nothing but winter boots . . . all left footed. Ve vere hungry again." The flames of the fire highlight his face. His eyes look far away, into a terrible time.

"I vas captured and put in a British prison camp. I escaped and returned to my village. Da same people there . . . da same ones that cheered me . . . spat upon me and threatened to turn me in if I didn't leave. I starved again." His voice sounds as brittle as the two steel blades that he'd sharpened.

"God, that was terrible. What did you do?" I asked.

"I stole a white sheet off a laundry line and skis and hid in da mountains. I became a smuggler." He pokes the fire again.

"Why the white sheet?" I ask.

"Vhen da border patrols chased me, I would lay in the snow and cover myself with da sheet. They never catch me."

"What did you smuggle?" I look at him and wonder if I could have survived what he'd been through.

"Anything da people want. Cigarettes . . . anything I could carry in my pack . . . something I could trade for food."

We fall silent, staring into the fire. My mind is a turmoil. Here I am in the mountains with a former SS officer, a German soldier, whom I'd been taught to hate, yet I can empathize with him. I simply can't conceive of going through his experiences.

"So, how did you get here?" I ask.

"An organization of former officers. I vas trained as a skilled mechanic, and after working in post-war Germany for a large company, they had jobs available in Canada. So, I am here."

Later, lying in my sleeping bag watching the stars move across the inky sky, I fight mixed emotions. It dawns on me, perhaps for the first time, that everything is not just black or white, good or evil, but that life is far more complex than I want it to be. Every man's life contains many shades of gray between those two poles.

Sleeping next to me in that vast mountain wilderness is a man who had been an officer in the SS, the most dreaded element of a hateful regime. He'd been a killer, yet here he is, volunteering to guide me to a bull elk in order to pay me back for saving his dog, Heidi. The Big Dipper traverses the entire skyline before sleep covers my disturbed mind.

The next morning I spot a lone bull elk cross a barren mountain saddle and drop into the head of a long drainage. We climb through jack-strawed, downed timber until we find a game trail that threads through ancient spruce trees next to a small stream.

On the way down, Fritz bugles, but we hear no answer. It's noon, windless, and so hot that we sweat even when we stop next to the stream. Flies and other insects, awakened from the cold, buzz and make us slap and wave.

"It's too hot. Da bull's bedded down in the shade. We eat," Fritz says as he swings his pack to the ground and takes out the sausage and cheese.

I sit next to him and gag down yet another piece of sausage and cheese that's starting to get slimy.

"Could I try out your bugle?" I ask.

"Ya. Von't hurt. Da bull's bedded down. Too hot."

His pronunciation of "won't" as "von't" reminds me of last night's conversation. I'd never know what I'd have done under similar circumstances . . . if I had had the power of choice. I remember the old Indian saying, "Don't judge a man until you've walked in his moccasins."

I place Fritz's elk bugle on my lips and blow a scream. Upstream, close, the bull elk bellows a response . . . a scream and series of grunts.

Fritz leaps up, wrenches his bugle from my hands, points at me, then a nearby stump. He grabs his rifle and pack and jogs back up the trail away from the bull. I creep behind the rotten stump, place a broadhead on my longbow, and listen to the enraged bull bellow again, even closer. He's on the move.

I hear Fritz bellow from up the trail. Immediately, the bull answers with a series of growling grunts. I see movement. The bull's rack appears over the top of the stump. I tense, ready to pull back the string.

The bull walks into sight. He stops and extends his neck and issues a scream that cuts through my mind. The scream ends in a series of grunts, and he humps and urinates on the back of his front legs. I pick a hair on the spot I want to hit low on his chest and began a slow draw. He takes another step up the trail.

I feel the back of the broadhead against my finger and wait for the bull to take one more step so his right leg will be forward to expose his chest. He takes a step forward, drops his head to smell my foot-scent on the trail, and I loose my arrow. It flies true and buries itself in his chest. He spins to the left, takes eight steps, stops, wavers, then topples dead.

I'm standing over the five-by-six-point bull when Fritz jogs up. His face is split by a crooked toothy grin. We whoop and holler. He slaps me on the back and dances a jig and takes off his hat and scratches his head. Then he becomes serious. He sticks out his hand and grips mine. His eyes bore into mine. His voice turns formal. "You save Heidi. Danka. Now ve're even."

# THE INITIATION—JOHN

"Dad!"

My thirteen-year-old son, John, shakes my shoulder to jolt me out of a midday nap. My eyes snap open.

"What?"

"I was carving with my new knife . . ." There's fear in his eyes when he holds his hand close to my face; it's a bloody mess.

"Oh, my God!" It's *déjà vu*; I know he's cut his finger off, like he did when he was three.

"I'm sorry. I'm sorry." His voice wavers.

"Don't worry. It'll be okay," I lie. I toss off my sleeping bag, swing my legs over the edge of the cot, and feel cold cross-cut wood planks under my bare feet. The top of my left arch stings with drops of my son's warm blood.

"Tish! Wake up," I scream. I can't look at John's hand. I remember what happened the last time.

69

My wife grasps the situation and races to John while I sprint from the bunk room to the kitchen to grab a dish towel. Tish wraps John's hand, then walks him into the kitchen where she pours cold creek water from a pail into a metal basin on the wood stove. She unwraps the towel and dunks his hand into the water, which swirls red.

I spot the knife, his twelfth birthday present, lying on the floor next to the table and stoop to pick it up. Drops of blood stain the wood floor but not the stainless steel blade.

I had presented the knife to John at lunch an hour ago, over Tish's objections that he was too young.

Folding the blade into its handle, I look for his finger on the red-and-white-checkered plastic table cover, but only see the partially carved stick upon which he'd been whittling. I toss it into the woodbin next to the stove.

"It's going to be okay, honey. Now hold your hand over the towel while I change water." Tish lobs the stained water from the basin out the open top of the Dutch door, and it arches over rough-hewn log steps to splash in the dirt.

I wonder if the smell of blood will draw a grizzly to our cabin tonight.

She pours fresh water into the basin, then lowers John's hand into it, gently.

"He cut it to the bone. Want to look?" Tish asks, giving me a look that says, "Please don't pass out this time."

"Yeah." I didn't like the hollow sound of my voice. I pray I won't faint like I did the time John was three and a child's folding chair collapsed and scissored off one of his fingers.

That time, Tish gathered up the end of John's finger, stuck it back on, wrapped it in her sweater, and rushed him to the hospital. When I ran into the Emergency Room, the doctor was sticking a long needle into his finger stub. I passed out on the floor, and they had to revive me before the doctor could sew up little John's finger.

Now I look at his cut. Nasty. To the bone.

"I've got to get him to town, to a doctor. Bandage it the best you can, Tish. I'll get the horses." I find Carol Luenberger taking a nap in the shade of an immense pine tree.

"Where's Robin?" I ask, after telling her about the accident. She says he's fixing tack in the horse shed. She then rushes into the cabin to help Tish.

I find Robin, our guide, and we saddle three horses. We can travel faster without Tish and Carol.

We mount up and say good-bye. Carol repeats the directions to the doctor's clinic. "He's a good doctor. Sews up knife cuts all the time, so John'll be just fine."

"You know the trail, Robin. You go first. John, keep your hand up against your chest and fall in behind Robin. I'll be right behind you, in case you need help."

"What kind of help will I need?" John asks.

"You might get light-headed," I say.

"Yeah, right. You're the one that faints, Dad."

We head down the mountain path toward the trailhead, where we'd left the truck.

Robin kicks his horse into a trot, ours follow.

"We can't trot! It'll make John's bleeding worse," I yell.

Robin slows to a fast walk. At this pace, it'll take several hours to get to the trailhead and another two hours to reach Fernie, the small village that's the center for lumbering and mining in this part of British Columbia.

I watch John riding ahead of me on Jughead, an aptly named horse. Damned thing is stubborn as a Missouri mule, and I remember the fight that John had getting the stupid thing to walk instead of jump over downed timber.

Robin had screamed at him time and again. "Control your horse! Don't let him jump over that log! He'll rip his guts out if he hits a snag."

I should have let John ride my horse. I was wrong in going along with Robin's idea that John would learn. Hell, no one could control that horse. Someone should use Jughead for bear bait.

Pretty soon we hit the crest of the valley and start on the long trail down the mountain through the forest.

"How ya holding up?" I ask John.

"Okay."

I try to move alongside of him, but John's horse, Jughead, begins to trot, so I back off.

"Hand throbbing yet, son?"

"Not bad."

Tough little kid. He'd done well on his first elk hunt. He'd watched our packhorse step on a hornet's nest that sent it bucking along a mountain ridge. Pots and pans and bedrolls flew off at the top of every buck, and cans of food spewed over the countryside. A mile later, the packsaddle finally slipped under the horse's belly and ropes tangled his legs to stop him.

It took most of the day to find our sleeping bags, pots, and other big items. We'd only planned an overnight, so we weren't carrying much food. We only found one can of beans.

Later that evening, we tied our horses to scrub pines and started glassing the valleys for elk. Even though the temperature was in the sixties, Tish, who was on her first mountain hunt, insisted on wearing long underwear, insulated pants, a wool shirt, sweater, heavy down coat and hood.

"There . . . there's a herd of elk drifting through that black timber next to the stream on the right side of the valley," I said as I watched patches of yellow elk hair slide between openings in the trees.

"I can't see a bull," John said.

"Yeah, but it's mating season, the bulls are in rut and should be gathering their harems. There's gotta be a big bull down with that herd. We'd better get down there and try to call him to us," I said.

"Let's go," Robin said, tucking his binoculars between the buttons of his shirt.

While John pulled his rifle out of his scabbard, I turned to Tish. "It's pretty hot. You'd better leave your coat here by the horses."

"I'll keep it on, thank you."

We scrambled over the side of the ridge and found that part of the mountain's forest had been the victim of a blow-down. Cyclone winds had leveled the trees, which jack-strawed across the slope. It was steep enough that we could simply step on the logs, then slide off the downside.

Forty minutes later, we were several hundred yards above the spot we'd seen the elk.

I motioned to John and whispered, "We'll hide behind that log. Mom'll stay back here with Robin. He'll call." We got into our ambush, and Robin started bugling and grunting. We called without success.

Forty-five minutes later Robin tapped me on the shoulder. "Must have spooked them. We'd better get back up to the horses before it's dark."

I tried to hide my disappointment. I really wanted John to have a chance to get a bull.

The jack-strawed timber that had been so easy to slide over when we came down became an obstacle course as we climbed back up. We had to lift our butts up on each log, then swing our legs over, stand up and climb to the next one, and repeat the process. It was hard, hot, sweaty work. It was particularly tough on Tish because she's short. Many of the logs were chest high but impossible for her to climb under because of the steepness of the slope.

Exhausted and overdressed, she was on the verge of heat stroke. She stopped and leaned against a log.

"I can't go another step!"

"Got to keep moving, honey. It's getting dark."

"I don't care. I'm not moving!"

Robin was a shadow moving upward a hundred yards above us. I looked at John. His eyes were wide as he watched the showdown.

"Look. You can't stay here all night. The temperature will drop to freezing.

"I'll freeze right here."

John's eyes grew wider. "Mom . . ."

"I can't move."

I reached for her arm. "We'll help you . . ."

Tish flailed at me with her fists. "I'm not going!"

I was shocked. It was the first time she'd hit me. John looked away, first at Robin's form high above us, then at the top of the ridge that was now silhouetted against the darkening sky.

"Look," I said with an edge to my voice, "the food is up there, our sleeping bags are up there and we're losing light. We can't stay here. Let's go."

"Go ahead!" She couldn't hold back tears.

"If you stay here, you'll die." I didn't know what else to say.

"I don't care if I die here."

I looked toward the ridge. The blown-down logs looked like white skeletons against the black of the mountainside. We didn't have much time, and we had no flashlights. I was in a Mexican standoff with my wife, and I felt responsible for her safety. John's worried face reminded me that the purpose of this first hunt was to teach him the joys of the hunt. Jeeze.

John scrambled close to his mother. "Mom, we've got to climb up there. We'll go slow and take our time."

Tish saw the worried look on his face and wiped away her tears. "You're right. Let's go." She tossed her coat to me.

He helped her up onto the next log and looked at me. I gave him a thumbs-up.

An hour later, in starlight, we crested the ridge to see that Robin had a small fire going with a bubbling can of baked beans tucked into its side. We were emotionally and physically exhausted. I unrolled our sleeping bags, looked at the millions of stars, and remembered my second objective of the trip . . . Tish and I could use our zip-together sleeping bags for the first time.

"I'll zip our bags together, honey," I said.

She didn't even look up. "Are you out of your mind?"

Now, a week later, rushing John down the mountain to the doctor, I grin when I remember John's laughter.

We tie our horses to trees at the trailhead, hop in the truck and bounce our way over logging roads toward Fernie, the nearest town with a doctor.

"How do you feel, John?" I ask, dreading his answer. My imagination says that he'll lose his finger. It'll screw him up both physically and mentally; I can hear the taunts of his schoolmates: "Hey, Fingers!"; "Hi, Stumpy"; "Ya lost something . . ."

"I'm okay. It doesn't hurt." He sits between Robin, who is driving, and me and holds his injured hand next to his chest. The blood on his bandage is bright red and wet.

John has a high pain threshold; something that knocks me to my knees doesn't bother him, so I don't know if he's okay or not. I'm nauseated.

Fernie's a small town and there's no hospital. We stop once to ask directions before we find the doctor's office in an old dilapidated house. We sit in a musty waiting room that has turn-of-thecentury linoleum flooring. I look at the spots worn through to the floor, the peeling wallpaper, and the hanging lamp that contains one light bulb, and I wonder if we should have spent a couple more hours driving to a town with a hospital.

"Come in." The doctor stands in the door to his examining room.

Robin waits while John and I walk into the room.

"Sit up here, son, and let me see what you've got," the doc says.

"I cut my finger with a knife," John says.

I watch, trying to decide whether or not to let the doctor work on John.

"Nasty, but you didn't cut a tendon. You'll need some stitches," he says to John. He turns to open a tray containing needles and thread.

"Huh, his finger is pretty important. Think he should see a specialist?" I ask, while he threads the needle and prepares a hypodermic.

His head rotates toward me in slow motion, then he smiles. "Look, I know you're worried about your son. This is a mining and lumber area. Ninety percent of my business is either job-related or injuries from bar fights with knives. I'm a knife-cut specialist, and I can tell you that he'll be fine."

The doc stitches John's finger, then bandages it. After I pay him and he walks us to the door, he asks John, "Like to play football, son?"

"Yeah, I play quarterback," John replies.

The doc pats John's shoulder. "Well, don't worry about that finger, son. You'll probably be the starting quarterback of your high school team."

# THE INITIATION—SUE

"Would you mind zipping up your fly?" I ask the obese guy who waddles out of the bunk room past the wood stove.

"Huh? What's your problem?" the hunter asks.

I feel my jaw tense, and I roll to the balls of my feet. "I brought my twelve-year-old daughter to camp, and she's too young to see your dick."

"Oh." He stops next to the rough-hewn dining table and looks down. He looks like he's in his early forties. His block head is topped with wild black hair, and the skin of his neck piles into folds like stacked tires. He strains to look over his potbelly.

A piece of his red-and-black-plaid hunting shirt peeks out the opening in his pants. He can't reach straight down, but wraps his arms around the sides of his belly to reach his fly. Finally, his chubby fingers seize the zipper and yank it three-quarters of the way up before it binds. He can't see it, so he either figures he's zipped up or doesn't give a damn. I mentally name him "Slob."

"Hey!" Slob yells. "Chow's on. Let's eat so we can get out there and hunt!"

I hear movement in the bunk room. It must be the other half of this dynamic duo.

Slob sits down at the table, grabs a slab of thick-crusted bread, slaps butter on it, then stabs a slice of cold elk meat with his fork and throws it on his plate.

I see Carol Luenberger, Heinz's wife, leading my daughter Sue across the small meadow in front of the log cabin. Their arms are linked. Carol is a big-boned woman with a world-worn face offset by sparkling blue eyes. I feel bad that Sue will be exposed to Slob and his partner. It's a hell of a way to start her first hunt.

The bottom half of the Dutch door swings open when Sue and Carol walk in to the cabin.

"Daddy! Carol showed me where a baby moose licks the salt block. I saw his tracks, and Carol said we might see him soon."

I smile at her. "That's good, honey, but we'd better be careful, because there's nothing more dangerous than a mama moose."

"He's an orphan," Carol says, then looks at the backside of Slob who munches away on his improvised sandwich. "Lunch isn't quite ready."

"Don't make no difference to me," Slob mutters.

The other hunter walks into the room and sticks out his hand to introduce himself. Slob makes such a negative first impression, I don't pick up the new guy's name but mentally name him Buddy.

"So how's hunting been?" I ask him.

"Slow. Elk haven't started bugling yet." Buddy, a tall, spare man about Slob's age, slides onto the bench next to his partner and reaches for the meat platter.

Carol puts a bowl of lettuce salad on the end of the table. "It's been too hot, and the bulls aren't in rut."

"We've been here three days and haven't shot anything. I paid good money to shoot something," Slob says.

Carol looks at me and rolls her eyes.

I try not to say anything, but can't help myself. "You pay an outfitter for an opportunity for a fair-chase hunt in his area—"

"Bullshit, I pay him so I can kill something." Slob pours water from a plastic pitcher toward his glass and ignores what splashes on the table.

"Mind if we eat later, Carol? We need to take a walk to loosen up our sore legs." Part of it is the truth, we'd just ridden into camp, and Robin, our guide, is still taking our gear off the packhorses.

Carol nods. I wonder if she resents being left with Slob and Buddy, but I don't want Sue's first moments ruined by these guys. I motion Sue to follow me outside where we find Robin and another guide, Randy, sitting in the shade of a pine tree. They don't look anxious to go into the cabin, either.

We sit down with them in the duff, and ignoring the sap that will stick to my shirt, I lean against the bark of the pine tree and savor its shade.

Pine scent blankets us, and the midday stillness is broken only by the intermittent buzzing of a bee. Sue runs her fingers through loose pine needles, first arranging them in one pattern, then another.

A rhythmic breeze puffs away the heat of the sun, and we talk about hunting until Randy leaves for the barn to saddle up Slob's and Buddy's horses for the evening hunt. Robin rises to follow Randy, but I stop him.

"Sue and I are going to hang around camp this afternoon, Robin. If the elk aren't in heavy rut this heat will make them stay in the shadows until dark. We'll have a better chance in the morning." Besides, I don't want to push Sue too hard on her first day.

We watch Slob try to mount his horse. Swearing, he lifts his left leg high toward the stirrup only to have the horse step sideways. Slob's boot thuds against the dirt.

"Stupid goddamned horse!" After his third attempt, Robin holds the horse's head, while Randy guides Slob's foot into the stirrup, then grabs the guy's ass and heaves. Slob's flaccid body flops onto the saddle, and Randy pushes his right leg to the other side. Sue grins at Carol, who covers her smile with a weathered hand.

They follow Randy down the trail, and we shout "Good luck," hoping to scare any nearby elk out of their way.

We walk back to the cabin to unpack, and when I pass through the door I'm surrounded by the smell of something baking: sugar and flour and fruit. I grin. Carol always spoils me. After spreading out our sleeping bags and hanging our clothes on wall pegs, we join Carol and Robin at the dinner table by the window.

Carol gets up, grabs a hot pad, and opens the wood stove's oven door. We're flooded with bakery scent. My mouth waters. Straightening, Carol turns and walks toward us, holding a golden-brown cherry pie in front of her ample bosom like a trophy.

"Susie, did you know your Daddy loves pie?" She grins and puts the pie down on the table in front of me.

"He sure does." Sue grins at me with an "I won't tell Mom" look.

I inhale its sweet aroma and look at the sugar sparkling on top of the golden crust. Carol is one of the few women in the world who knows how to make crisp crusts. My wife, Tish, is another expert. Love 'em both.

I finish my second piece of pie and groan with pleasure. There are still three pieces left for later.

"How's John's finger?" Carol asks, referring to last fall, when my son John cut his finger to the bone with his birthday knife. She puts her coffee cup down.

"When I saw that doctor's stitching job, I thought his finger would be disfigured, but it turned out great. He's playing quarterback on the football team, and he throws the ball well. You can't even tell it'd been cut."

"That's wonderful. That doctor gets a lot of practice sewing up drunks from the mining and lumber camps. I thought it would be okay."

"Yeah, but I was sure worried when we rode out of here. Speaking of riding, I don't see that horse John rode last year in your string." I vow to not let Sue ride a lousy horse.

"Jughead?" Robin asks.

"Yeah, Jughead." I lift my cup and swig hot sweetened tea.

"Heinz shot Jughead this spring, used him as bear bait." Robin grins.

Sue's eyes widen. She's not sure if Robin is serious or spoofing.

"Did Jughead draw in any bears?" I put my cup down and eye the remaining pie. Too early. If I have another piece now it wouldn't be polite.

"Naw." Robin strikes a match on the bottom of the table and lights a Player cigarette, then blows smoke toward the ceiling.

"Jughead was even ornery after death. I can hardly wait to kid Heinz about that darned horse. When'll Heinz be here?" I ask.

"He's due to bring supplies up from the lower camp tomorrow." Robin takes a last draw, then stubs his cigarette out.

"Look!" Carol points out the window. We watch a young moose slide out of the tree shadows and walk in a stiff-legged moose stride toward the salt block.

"Oh, he's cute, Daddy!" Sue stands up and leans against the window for a better view.

I get my binoculars and walk to the Dutch door. "Come over here, Sue. Take a close look through my glasses."

She rests the binoculars on top of the lower door. "He has the prettiest brown eyes!"

We watch the baby moose until his taste is sated and he turns and disappears into the pines.

Sue and I manage to eat and be in our bunks before Slob and Buddy return from their hunt. We watch flickering shadows on the bunk room ceiling caused by the kitchen lantern and listen to Slob bitch about not killing anything, what a lousy outfit this is, and how he's getting ripped off.

"Remember, we have a young lady in camp," Carol warns them when they push back from the table to head for the bunk room.

I smile. I've never thought of my little girl as a lady before.

Slob's snoring isn't regular, it starts soft, builds to a crescendo, then climaxes with a loud snort. I strain to hear him breathing, emotionally torn between hoping that he's stopped breathing, then feeling guilty at the thought. Surely, someone loves him.

When Robin gets back from wrangling the horses for the morning hunt, I tell him that I want to hunt close enough to the camp to get back for lunch. I've decided to take it real easy, so Sue'll enjoy her first wilderness experience.

Under the stars, Robin and Randy heave Slob on his horse, then we mount up and follow them down the trail. Saddle leather creaks, horseshoes clink against rocks, and in the far distance a pack of coyotes howl. Starlight creates a contrast between silvery shapes and black shadows where the mind senses grizzly bears and wolves lurking.

I tuck the collar of my down coat around my neck and shiver from the pre-dawn cold. There's a wide spot in the trail, and I nudge my horse next to Sue's and whisper, "You warm enough, honey?"

"Yes." The tentative sound of her whisper tells me that her mind has also imagined things lurking in black shadows.

Smiling, I rein my horse back into line. Good. That's one of the experiences I want to share with her.

I want her to understand that our so-called "civilized" existence has left us far removed from the reality of life.

I want her to experience the hardship of the hunt, the difficulty of getting close to a wild animal who, unlike its feedlot cousin, has a chance at freedom.

I want her to know the exhilaration and deep sorrow of the kill.

I want her to watch eyes glaze in death, feel warm blood on her hands, smell feces and guts, and feel sweat trickle down her face and back when she cuts and packs the meat, skin, and antlers.

I want her to smell and taste elk tenderloin grilled on a fresh-cut alder branch over an open fire, to feel the warm meat fill her tummy.

I want her to understand that we've come so far from reality that we hire others to do our killing, hire others to gut, scale, and pluck, hire others to cut and wrap.

That material things, the "sophistication" of our lives with fancy clothes, stereos, computers, cars, houses, those "things" that we strive for and thrive in, are nothing but window dressings for the stark reality of life. We, like all species on this planet, depend on and kill other species in order to live.

I'm shaken from my thoughts when I see Robin rein his horse off the main trail onto a path that traverses up the side of the mountain. Three other black shapes, Randy, Slob and Buddy, plod forward on the main trail below. I feel sorry for Randy, but thankful we've left them.

The trail switchbacks until it breaks free of treeline near a ridge that overlooks another drainage. We tie the horses in a clump of windblown dwarf pines and scramble to the top of the ridge, where we find shelter from the pre-dawn breeze in a group of boulders. We hide among their massive bulk and set up our spotting scopes to glass the valley below for elk when the sky lightens.

Resting shoulder-to-shoulder, silent, we watch stars disappear, the black night sky turn to leaden gray, then marvel at the first fiery rays of sun that streak the heavens. Far below, the hoots of a great horned owl are answered by the howl of a lone wolf. I feel Sue shiver and sink deeper into her coat.

I raise my elk bugle and give a long, high-pitched scream that ends in a series of grunts. We listen for an answer in the silence of the valley.

The sun rises, painting the mountaintops with alpenglow. We glass the valley below for yellow elk slipping through the dark trees along the stream bank. Nothing.

We glass and bugle for several hours. I ask Robin if we should move.

"By the time we get to another ridge, it will be hot and the elk will have bedded down. Better to stay here. There has to be a herd down there someplace."

"Yeah, if the wolf hasn't spooked them out." I wonder if it's a single wolf or a pack.

The sun's rays warm us and soon I'm nodding. My head falls against my chest and my eyes snap open. Robin has stretched out in the sun and is snoring. Sue looks at me.

"There's nothing happening down below, honey. We got up early. You might want to take a nap in the sun. I'm going to." I move to a flat patch covered by wild strawberry plants and snuggle flat in the sweet-smelling place while the sun warms me into a sound sleep.

The sun is high overhead when I wake up and look around. Robin is sprawled on his back, his head rests on his down coat. Sue's coat lies on the ground near me, but she is missing.

Panic surges, tightening my chest. I struggle to my feet and look up and down the ridge. Nothing.

I walk through the boulders, thinking she's resting on the other side, out of sight. She's not there.

My throat constricts and my stomach heaves when I think of terrible alternatives: lost, starvation, bears, wolves, mauling.

"What's wrong?" Robin, having heard my footsteps, leans on his elbows.

"Sue's missing!" I run to the edge of the ridge and look down the slope. Two hundred yards below, there's a spot of blue below a long spit of sand. It moves. I raise my binoculars, focus and spot Sue's blue and black checked shirt. My breath gushes out. She's bent over, writing large letters in the sand. I can see the two short braids that stick out from each side of her golden hair. Imagining danger, I scan the area around her for bears, wolves, or other stalking predators. Nothing. I grab my rifle and hurry down to her.

"Hi, Daddy." She smiles at me.

"You had me worried, honey. I thought you were lost."

"You were snoring, so I just came down here to mess around in the sand." She drops the stick she's using to write on the ground.

"It can be dangerous to get separated in the mountains, honey. I woke up and couldn't find you and got worried." That's a lie, I think. I was scared shitless.

"I'm sorry, Daddy."

"That's okay, but let's stick together from now on." I look at the letters she'd spelled out in the sand. It's a boy's name. I'm shocked.

"You were sleeping, and I was pretty bored." She looks on the verge of tears.

"Yeah, I understand." I point to the name in the sand. "Who's that?"

"Just a boy." She grins.

"Anyone I know?" Amazement pushes aside my shock.

"No, just a boy at home."

Holy cow, she's starting to think about boys. "Well, we'd better climb back up to the horses. We need to get back to camp for lunch."

Slob, Buddy, and Randy are sitting at the table, backs to the wall, eating lunch when we arrive.

"Any luck?" I ask.

"Naw. No damned animals here. Nothing to shoot at." Slob, sitting on the end of the bench, wipes his mouth with the back of his hand, then looks out the window.

Carol rolls her eyes at me again, then nods to the warming oven above the wood stove. I open the door and spy the remaining three pieces of cherry pie. One for Sue, Robin, and me. Two for me if Sue starts thinking about that boy and declines a piece.

We sit at the table and start lunch.

"Oh look, Daddy! The baby moose is at the salt block again." Sue scoots to her knees for a better view.

I stand up and look over Robin's head, and Slob scuttles away from the table and hurries to the bunk room. Probably to get his binoculars for a close-up view.

The little fellow licks the salt, then raises his head and looks straight ahead. Even without binoculars, I can see his tongue licking his nose. His ears flick away flying insects.

Carol's voice startles me. "You can't do that!"

I turn to see her looking at the door. Slob, balancing on one knee, rests his rifle on the top of the lower Dutch door, shoulders it, and looks through the scope. His finger tightens on the trigger.

"Hey!" I shout at him and trip on the bench trying to stop him. Too late.

The explosion deafens us. The baby moose falls on its side, legs twitching.

"I got him!" Slob struggles to his feet.

"You son-of-a-bitch!" My urge to deck the guy is tempered by his loaded rifle, which is now pointed at the floor between us.

"What the hell's wrong with you?" Slob's wild eyes lock with mine.

"First, that was the camp pet. Second, it was a baby. Third, you just shot an illegal animal. You're disgusting." If I move Slob might do something really stupid.

"I paid my hard-earned money to kill something. And I just killed something." Defiant, Slob doesn't move the rifle.

Sue is crying.

"Jeeze," Randy moans.

Carol's fists are on her hips, her eyes ice. "Put that rifle down and go out there and take a good look at what you just did."

Slob looks at her, then turns to us. He looks at Buddy, but gets no support. He wrenches open the door, cradles his rifle in his arm, steps out of the cabin, and stalks across the grass to stand above the still form of the little moose.

"I'm sorry . . ." Buddy's voice trails off as he follows Slob. When he's ten yards away from his hunting partner, Slob jerks the rifle to his shoulder and fires another round into the dead moose. Its small body spasms.

"We've got to get that guy out of camp." My hands are shaking.

"Heinz will be here soon. He'll take care of it."

"Robin, let's you, Sue, and me get out of here. I don't trust myself with that guy." I walk into the bunk room to help Sue gather her things, while Robin goes for the horses.

I walk back into the kitchen. Randy and Carol are standing by the door, watching Slob and Buddy stand over the baby moose.

Buddy has his hand on Slob's shoulder, and as we watch, they walk into the woods on the far side of the meadow, leaving the black corpse of the baby moose lying by the salt block.

"You two going to be okay?" I ask. "We'll stay, if you need support."

"You get Sue out of here. That guy's going to have remorse. He won't cause any more trouble." Carol's eyes are still cold.

An hour later, Robin, Sue, and I sit on a high ridge several miles from camp. I try to explain to her that most hunters have a good sense of ethics, but there is a minority of bad guys who have no business being in the woods, and Slob is the worst I've met. I'm sorry that she had to be exposed to him.

She says she understands, but I wonder and I feel depressed. There are so many good things that I want her to experience, and she has to be in the same camp as Slob.

"Look at the trail leading out of camp," Robin says.

I raise my binoculars and watch a packtrain wind down the trail from camp to the trailhead. Even from this distance I can tell Heinz leads three packhorses, followed by Buddy, then Slob, who looks like a blob on his horse.

"Good for Heinz and good riddance." Robin hands his binoculars to Sue.

We hunt until dark, then ride back to camp where Carol has hot chili, corn bread, and another pie waiting. This one is peach, yet its aroma doesn't cast out the gloom that's settled over my mind.

"Any trouble?" Robin looks at Carol as he fishes a pack of Players cigarettes out of his shirt pocket.

"No. Heinz arrived soon after you left. When he heard the story, he told those guys to pack up, their hunt's over. The killer complained that they had four more days on their hunt, but Heinz told him he'd broken the game laws of British Columbia.

He had a choice, either leave now or be tossed in jail. He reminded the guy that it takes a lot of time and money to get out of a foreign jail. The guy sulked but kept his mouth shut."

"What happened to the baby moose?" Sue asks Carol.

"Randy packed the moose a few miles down valley and put him far off the trail. He won't go to waste."

"What do you mean?" Sue ladles hot water from the well on the side of the wood stove into a wash basin.

"Bears and wolves are always hungry." Carol hands Sue a wash cloth.

"It's too bad." Sue scrubs her face and hands.

"Sue, that moose was probably too young to survive the winter. It needed its mother for warmth and protection." I don't know that for sure, but it sounds better than leaving the baby moose where it was. Maybe I'm trying to sugarcoat reality.

After dinner and before hitting the sack, we watch a full moon spring from the tops of the forest to bathe the meadow an iridescent silver. A pack of coyotes yelp in the distance. Life in the mountains settles into its usual rhythm.

Moonlight beams through the window of the bunk room when Sue gently shakes my shoulder. "Daddy, I think I'm going to be sick."

"Let's get outside, honey." Oh, my God. She stands next to my bunk, covered by her full-length cotton nightgown. I swing out of my sleeping bag and lead her past the woodstove in the kitchen, open the door, and hold her shoulders as we walk into the silver grass in front of the cabin.

She starts to gag, and I hold her tummy and forehead when she vomits. Its smell violates the scent of the forest and meadow. Moonlight casts our shadows against the grass. Our bare feet are cold and wet from the dew on the grass.

"Oh, Daddy!"

"Go on, honey. Get it all out. You'll feel better." I watch another stream of partially digested chili eject onto the earth.

"I'm bleeding, Daddy!" She gags again.

"No, honey, that's just the color of the chili." I raise my head to suck in a deep breath of cold air.

"No! No, I'm bleeding." She sobs.

"Honey, that's just the color of the chili in the moonlight." I look at the forest beyond the meadow.

"*No!* It's not the chili, Daddy. I'm bleeding . . . between my legs!"

I stagger and hold myself up on my little girl . . . my little lady . . . this woman. I'm going to faint. It can't be. She's too young for this to be happening. Here. Now. With me. Where's Tish? Has Tish talked to her about these things? "Uh . . . what do you mean, honey?"

"I think I have my first period, Daddy." Sue's voice has a subtle tone only grown women use on men. Men sense such sounds.

I'm shocked speechless, and stagger to recover. "Do you . . . did your mother send anything with you?"

"Maybe you should wake up Carol, Daddy."

"Good idea!" I run back to the cabin and shout for Carol, who takes charge of the situation.

Robin lights the lantern and tosses sticks of wood in the stove's firebox. He grins at me as I sit on the bench by the table. "Looks like you could use a hot tea . . . or something stronger."

He puts the teapot on the stove, then pulls a bottle of brandy from behind a shelf, pours half a glass and sets it in front of me. I stare at it.

Carol and Sue join us at the table. I notice Sue is wearing one of Carol's nightgowns under her coat.

"Are you okay, Sue?"

Her smile seems different now, older, wiser. "Are *you* okay, Daddy?"

"Yeah, of course," I lie and take a swig of brandy. My little girl, my little lady, has turned into a woman. She . . . she can bear a child.

"Miracle," I mutter as I push the empty brandy glass to Robin for a refill.

# THE INITIATION—TOM

"At least you don't have to guide Slob this year, Randy." I grin at the young man who sits tall on a sorrel horse that stands sixteen hands.

"That's a blessing. I darned near quit guiding after that experience." He pulls his sweat-stained black cowboy hat tight on his head. It's his last chance. Both hands will be full for the next hour or so—left hand holding the reins to his horse, his right holding the lead rope to the packhorses.

"Yeah, I'm glad you didn't. It'll be fun hunting with you." I hand him the lead rope that is attached to the halter of the first horse in our packstring.

I walk along the line of horses, checking to make sure the lead ropes from the packsaddles are untangled. In the process, I inspect the canvas-covered packs, each lashed with a diamond hitch. No sense in starting out with a loose pack, then having to repack it on a steep mountain slope.

I pat Tish's knee. She looks small on her horse. "You ready, honey?"

"Yes." Tish's answer is qualified. She is a terrific athlete, but uncomfortable on a horse.

Son Tom swings into his saddle and walks his horse next to Sharon, the cook. He grins and says something to her that makes her laugh.

"Buttering up the cook?" I ask.

"She promises to give me the first piece of pie." A smile splits his face. Even at thirteen, he's comfortable around all kinds of people. Must be because he's the youngest. Or maybe he's happy because we took him out of school for a week for his initiation hunt.

I check the cinch to my saddle one last time, then swing up and try to get my toe in the right stirrup while my horse jigs a stiff-legged dance that makes Tish frown with worry. "Let's move 'em out!"

Tom shouts, "Whoop! Whooop!" He must have seen that in some old cowboy movie, but I like the sound. It's appropriate. Maybe I'll use it sometime.

Randy leads the packstring up the trail, followed by Sharon, Tom, then Tish. I ride drag so if there's trouble I can give quick help.

The horses scramble up a steep slope and I watch Tish, who looks tense in the saddle, but I remind myself it's been four years since she'd been on a horse. Six years since our first trip, initiating our oldest son, John, into the hunt.

"You okay, honey?" I ask her.

"You don't have to keep asking me that." She's sensitive, and I vow to keep my mouth shut.

Randy leans over his saddle horn while he reins his horse to the left around a switchback and spurs him up another steep spot in the trail. He holds the lead rope with his gloved hand high over his horse's rump so it won't slip under its tail.

The first packhorse pulls back, forcing Randy to absorb the shock with his body. By the time the last packhorse makes the turn, he's leaning so far back across his horse's rump he looks like a rodeo bronc rider.

I grin at Randy who passes ten yards above me.

He grins back. "I'm glad we have the camp to ourselves this year."

"Yeah, me too." I'll miss Heinz and Carol who are taking care of a bighorn sheep hunter at low camp. Carol was a godsend during Sue's hunt. I'll miss her pies, but she assured me that she'd taught Sharon her secret recipes, so the trip won't be a bust.

"Listen to that, John." Randy nods down the mountain.

"I hear it." A logging truck's engine grinds as the driver nears a hill. The sound rips through the peaceful silence, and while I understand we've got to have more lumber to supply this over-populating world, I'm saddened by the intrusive noise.

"Every year the lumber and mining companies cut the road farther into the wilderness. Our ride to high camp will be forty-five minutes shorter this year." Not expecting an answer, Randy turns in his saddle to concentrate on the trail ahead.

I wish I could see Tom's eyes when we ride into high camp, but he's off his horse and has it tied to a hitching rail and is helping Randy with the packstring. We unpack the horses, haul supplies and our gear to the cabin, then Randy, Tom, and I unsaddle the horses and brush them out while Tish and Sharon put the supplies away.

"Grab your rifle and a box of cartridges, Tom, and let's sight it." I walk into the kitchen and cut the side of a cardboard box for a target.

We walk through the meadow in front of the cabin to the salt block.

"Here's where that slob hunter murdered the baby moose." We talk about ethics of the hunt, and Tom understands more than I thought.

"When am I going to sight in my rifle?" Tom's impatient and focused.

"In a minute. If you have an opportunity for a shot at a bull elk, it's important to place your shot accurately, so the kill is clean and quick."

"Yeah, I know." He was ready. We'd been over this many times before, when we'd shot together in Illinois. At night we'd go over shot placement angles and no-shot scenarios.

I tack the cardboard on a log. "Now, let's step off a hundred paces and see how well you can hit it."

I watch carefully while he fills the magazine with cartridges, closes the bolt without a shell in the chamber, then, just to make sure, snaps the safety on. He drops to the ground, lines up the target, chambers a shell, aims, and fires. I watch a round black hole appear in the cardboard.

"Good job. You're ready. Now we'll have to find a bull elk and get him to stand broadside like that log."

We hunt for four days without success. In the middle of the morning of the fourth day we find ourselves riding along a ridge that looks familiar. The wind blows the long grass in undulating waves.

Tish jerks her reins to force the head of her horse up from eating grass. She's riding a real grass hog, and grass hogs can be dangerous because when they're eating they often stumble. "This looks familiar. Is it . . ."

"Yeah, you should recognize it. We're on the ridge where we camped out with Johnny. Right down there is where we chased the elk." I point at the mountainside where downed trees were jack-strawed.

"I remember." Tish's eyes said she hoped we wouldn't see elk in that valley today.

"Know what Heinz and the guides named this part of the ridge?" I grin.

"No." Her eyes narrow, as if she knows what's coming.

"Beat 'em Up Ridge. Named it for us." I laugh.

Tish's laugh sounds hollow, as if she doesn't appreciate the humor in my lie.

Tom reins back to us. He's heard our conversation. "Is this where it happened?"

Tish shoots me a warning look. Her horse has its nose buried in the long grass.

"What?" I ask with feigned innocence.

"Where Mom . . . lost it?" Tom grins.

"Yep." I pull my Stetson brim down low over my eyes to keep the wind from blowing it off, or maybe to hide my eyes.

"There are two sides to that story." Tish jerks her horse's head up, hard. Long, succulent grass dangles from its mouth.

Laughing, I point to a spot farther down the ridge, "Over there is where your mother refused to let me zip our sleeping bags together. They now call that 'Frigid Ridge.' "

"John . . ." Tish's horse crumples to the ground under her. She's standing up in her stirrups, in the grass. The horse raises its head in a desperate attempt to breathe. It's going to roll and pin Tish under it.

"Get off! Get away from your horse." I jump off my horse, run to her, and help her away from her horse.

Tom's off his horse and holds my reins, preventing my horse from running away.

Tish's horse rolls to its side, and I strip off its bridle and pull the grass-choked bit from its mouth.

Randy rides back, dismounts, and hurries to us. "You okay? What's wrong with the horse?"

"It was eating and the grass got wrapped around the bit and choked him. He'll be all right now." The horse rolls to all fours, then lunges up. I slip the end of a rein around his neck.

Tom walks up close to help me put the bridle back on. Grinning, he whispers, "Saved by a choking horse."

"Let's not talk about 'Frigid Ridge,' " I whisper, while latching the neck strap.

"Let's ride over to the west side to get out of this wind. We'll find a place to have lunch." Randy swings back into his saddle, while Tom gives Tish a leg up.

We tie our horses in a clump of scrub pine on the leeward side of the ridge, pull our sack lunches out of our saddlebags, and find a soft, flat spot to sit down.

"Look! Wild strawberries." Tish holds up a tiny red fruit between her fingers. It disappears in her mouth.

There's nothing sweeter in the whole world that a ripe wild strawberry. My mouth waters. Ignoring my sandwich, I roll onto my hands and knees and look for strawberries.

Tom watches Tish, Randy, and me crawling like crazed bears. He takes off his hat and scratches his head.

"Here, Tom, try them." Tish hands him five or six tiny berries.

"Pretty small." He looks at them, pops them in his mouth, then grins. He, too, falls to his hands and knees and begins to pick and eat wild strawberries.

We're soon full and roll onto our backs and watch clouds puff across the intense blue sky. We make out different animal shapes in the clouds and laugh when no one else can see what we see.

I think about all the things I wanted to teach my kids about hunting. Words well up in me.

"You know, I think that as a society we've lost the sense of humility when we receive the gift of life by the death of another, whether it be vegetable, fish, fowl, or animal. That's particularly true when we go to the supermarket and toss a pre-processed, shrink-wrapped package into our grocery cart. Or go to a McDonalds, Long John Silvers, or Taco Bell."

No one answers and I turn my head and look at Tom. He's gazing at the clouds. I don't know if he's heard me, but I plow on.

"One of the reasons I hunt every year is that it's a ritual that reminds me that all species are connected and the taking of life to sustain our own is the reality of life's process."

I wait for a response, but there is none. Enveloped by the smell of wild fruit, listening to the buzzing of bees, and warmed by the sun, we nap.

"What time is it?" Randy asks the sky.

I look at my watch. "Quarter to three."

"We'd better saddle up and head toward camp. There's a valley we can hunt on the way back." Randy stands up and walks toward the horses.

An hour and a half later, we sit on another ridge overlooking a shallow valley dotted with patches of timber and meadows. Randy bugles, and we listen to silence.

I tense when I spot something moving along a far ridge and raise my binoculars. "Damn!"

"What?" Randy swings his glasses to the same ridge.

"See a bull, Dad? Or a bear?" Tom's excited.

"No. What I see is a Jeep with two guys in it."

Randy spots them. "Yeah, the mining company punched all kinds of exploratory roads up here this summer. They must be on one."

I feel a sense of loss at this ever-increasing pressure on wild places. Before I can articulate my thoughts, we hear a bull scream in the little valley below and swing our glasses toward the valley.

"See him?" I sweep the valley floor, but can find nothing.

"No, not yet." Randy is scanning the black timber on the far side.

The bull screams again. It's a high-pitched scream that ends with a low, coughing series of grunts.

"There he is!" Tom points to a spot in the valley just below us. We'd all been looking too far away to spot him.

The bull stands on the edge of a meadow in the shade of tall pines. Four cows feed through the trees toward the meadow. His harem. He screams again, then struts into the meadow and tears up a sapling with his antlers.

"He's hot." I look at our stalking possibilities. The bull is not more than three quarters of a mile away, but if all four of us try to sneak down to within rifle range, the cows will spot us, or wind us, or hear us. Too many people, too much scent, too much noise.

I want to be with Tom when he stalks the bull, but I figure Randy is more experienced. "I'll wait with Tish and watch from here. Good luck, guys."

Tom slings his rifle over his shoulder and follows Randy through the trees down the mountainside toward the elk. When they disappear, I watch the bull run from one end of the meadow to the other, chasing an imaginary opponent. He raises his head high and screams his challenge.

I wonder if Randy's earlier bugle stirred the bull out of his day bed.

The bull is feeding on the far side of the meadow when we hear Randy bugle. The bull's head snaps up, and he runs toward his cows, who are staring back at the timber. He herds up his cows and drives them across the meadow, away from the challenger.

"Damn!" I mutter.

"What's wrong?" Tish is looking through her binoculars.

"That bull thinks Randy is a bigger bull and he's going to run off with his cows. Tom won't have a chance."

We watch the bull push his cows into the dark timber on the far side of the meadow, then we spot Tom and Randy using downed timber and alder bushes for cover as they skirt the up-wind side of the meadow. Randy bugles again.

The bull answers and trots back out of the timber toward Tom and Randy, who are crouched behind a jumble of downed trees. The bull tears at the ground with his antlers, then throws a clump of grass and dirt over his shoulder. I figure Tom must be shaking pretty badly by now.

The bull is well within range, but he's standing head-on to Tom. I pray he remembers to only take a good broadside shot. Finally, the bull turns and walks broadside, then stops.

As we watch, the bull falls to the ground, then we hear one rifle shot echo across the valley. The scene is frozen while Tom waits, ready to shoot again if the bull rises. He doesn't.

Tom and Randy cautiously walk across the meadow to the bull. Tom touches the bull's eye with the muzzle of his rifle. The bull would blink at the touch if he's alive. He doesn't.

We see Randy shake Tom's hand, then Tom turns and waves at us.

Tish and I lead the four horses down to the kill site and congratulate Tom and Randy. It's a nice five-point bull. A fine trophy for Tom's first hunt.

We take pictures before starting the work—the gutting, cutting, caping. We'll tie the front and hindquarters to our saddles and lead our horses through the starlit night back to camp. Tom can shoulder the elk rack until he tires, then I'll carry it.

Tom's fingers stroke the long antler tines.

"How do you feel, son?" I'm curious to see if he's learned a lesson from his first big game kill.

"At first, I was real excited, but now I'm sad." Tom looks at his feet.

I wrap my arm around his shoulders and give him a rough man-hug. "That's the way you should feel, son. You're learning."

# PRINCE RUPERT
# IMAGES

"Did you know this town is the Alcoholic Capital of Canada?" I ask my hunting buddy, Doc England, who sits on the next bar stool.

"How'd you learn that?" he asks.

"Bartender told me while you were on the phone," I say. After four days sitting in a dingy hotel room, waiting for the worst storm in the past twenty years to blow itself out, we've gone to a bar for a change of scenery.

"I called our guide. He said the forecast is for better weather. We might be able to leave tomorrow or the next day. He'll call and let us know." Doc tips his bottle of beer back and orders another.

"Hope it's tomorrow. We've lost too many hunting days," I say, impatient to board the sixty-five-foot salmon trawler to cruise the fjords toward Alaska and hunt coastal grizzlies. Commonly called brown bear, these griz feed on salmon and grow to immense size.

A drunk spots easy marks, staggers over, and with slurred speech we hardly understand, hits us up for a drink. We refuse. His next utterance is clear: "Bastards!" He stumbles away to mooch from others.

The bar stinks of stale beer. A cloud of cigarette smoke obscures the ceiling. A group of five guys, who could be lumberjacks, play poker at a round table near the door, while two out of the eight customers sitting at the bar sleep on folded arms.

A pock-faced woman with long raven hair weaves across the floor toward the Wurlitzer jukebox. Two men follow her like bucks in rut. She steadies herself against the music machine, takes a swig of beer, then bends to squint at the song selections. The man in the torn wool plaid shirt wiggles his pelvis against her butt and gropes her breasts. She laughs.

I look at my watch. It's ten-thirty in the morning.

# DOC'S ARRANGEMENTS

We chug out of Prince Rupert's harbor in the salmon trawler that will be our bear hunting camp. It's a three-hour run through heavy seas before we find smooth water on the lee side of the coastal islands.

Steep timbered islands, tops crowned by wisps of white mist, slip past. Bald eagles sit on branches of fir trees that crowd the black water's edge. Seals frolic in the fjord, seagulls circle schools of fish, and we look for whales to break the surface. The dark landscape is broken by brilliant white glaciers. I feel in awe of this place and vow to one day share it with my wife, Tish.

We anchor in a cove, and the cook tosses a crab pot overboard to catch Alaskan king crabs for dinner.

"We'll take the jet boat up that river in the morning and float back looking for bear. When we spot one, we'll get on shore and stalk him to try to get a shot. If the river doesn't go down, we might have trouble getting up far enough for long floats." Our guide points out the window to the mouth of a swollen river disgorging swirling gray muck into the black ocean.

"Get your weapons and you can sight in on that floating log. It's about 125 yards." The guide turns to the wheelhouse to check a chart.

Doc and I go below to our cabin where he uncases his Winchester .270. I look at his rifle and think most hunters would be underpowered with that caliber, but Doc is a terrific shot. He'll do well.

"Did you tell the guide I shoot a bow?" I ask.

"I'm sure I did," Doc says, picking up a box of cartridges.

I leave my bow cased.

We go on deck and the guide and cook watch through binoculars while Doc rests his rifle on the boat's railing.

"Aim for that white spot on the left side of the log," the guide orders.

Doc squeezes off a shot and the white spot explodes.

"Good shot, Doc. Your rifle's sighted in just fine," the guide says.

Doc opens his bolt, catches his ejected cartridge, and stands up.

The guide turns to me. "Where's your weapon?"

"In its case under my bunk." I glance at Doc, who suddenly becomes interested in something on the shore.

"You gotta sight in before we go hunting," the guide says.

"I have to be a lot closer than that log before I'll shoot a bear." I notice Doc is still studying the shore.

"Look, get your weapon and sight it in." An impatient edge creeps into the guide's voice.

"Whatever you say." I go down to our room, uncase my longbow, put six arrows in my quiver, and walk back to the deck.

"What the . . . ?" The guide exclaims.

"My weapon." I hold it out to show him. He ignores it.

"Stop fooling around. Get your rifle, so you can sight in." A vein on the right side of his neck throbs.

I look at Doc. "You didn't tell him I was a bowhunter, did you?"

"Ah . . . I must have overlooked it." Doc flashes a little-boy grin. It's an engaging look, one that women, in particular, love.

I make a resolution to be in charge of booking our next hunt.

"I'm not taking you bear hunting if you're going to shoot that damned toy." The guide's hands ball into fists.

"This toy's killed a lot of big game animals," I retort.

"Not a brown bear." His remark isn't a question.

"No, not a coastal grizzly." I lean against the rail.

"I won't take you. It's too dangerous." He digs in.

"Look, there are salmon still spawning in the rivers, right?" I ask.

"Yeah, some leftovers," he admits.

"And bear feed on salmon?" I ask.

He looks at me like I'm some kind of smart-ass weirdo.

"Look, all you have to do is take me up the river to a feeder stream that contains salmon, and I'll find a tree to sit in. If one comes along, I'll decide whether or not it's safe to shoot."

"It's dangerous and I'm responsible." His tone weakens.

"I'll be above the reach of any bear. All you have to do is take the jet boat and drop me off and pick me up." I feel confident with my compromise.

"Okay, I'll drop you off, then take Doc upriver to hunt, and we'll pick you up when we return. Besides, since we were delayed by the storm, you've only got three days to hunt." The guide says.

The next morning, the guide, Doc, and I get into the jet boat and roar up a river, where they drop me off at a salmon-filled stream. I find a huge fir next to a bear trail along the stream and climb high and sit on a thick branch. I lean against the tree's trunk and watch salmon and eagles and more salmon.

That evening I hear the jet boat and expect to see the guide. It's the cook, armed with a short-barreled shotgun. He has a frightened look on his face.

"Where are the other guys?" I ask when I step into the boat.

"They came back early." The cook scans the bushes along the shore.

I wonder why I didn't hear the roar of their jet boat returning, then remember they floated back to the fjord.

I find Doc sitting at the ship's dining table nursing a tumbler of Scotch. "So, how was your hunt?"

"The river's so high that we can't get the jet boat far enough up to get a long float, so we can't cover enough of the country. And, because of the storm, the river will rise even higher." Doc looks depressed.

I don't blame him. The weather has screwed up our trip.

The guide dials the marine weather channel on the ship's radio, and we listen to the report of another huge storm forecast to hit the coast day after tomorrow.

"We'd better call 'er quits," the guide says. "We'll pull out at daybreak."

As we near the end of our storm-plagued trip, the spirits of the guide and cook improve each mile. Our spirits sink.

Docking at Prince Rupert, the guide offers a lower fee because of lost hunting days, and we write the hunt off to elements beyond our control.

At least I didn't have to sight in my weapon.

# POND LILLY

"Listen!" Son Tom's whisper slices through the damp night air of the river bottom.

We stop and listen to splashing, chasing, slapping, flapping, quaking; a chorus of mallards on Pond Lilly.

"Must be a thousand of them." John, my older son, stands close to me, while one hen bellows a series of provocative squawks.

"More like five thousand," Biz Ford, our duck hunting buddy, murmurs.

"Let's not spook them," I warn. We move toward the sounds that arouse men from warm beds in the middle of cold nights.

Following the beam of my light, we thread single file through cottonwoods and oaks. Gnarled trunks stretch high, their shadows swaying in the shaft of light.

"Look left!" John whispers.

Burning yellow eyes stare at us, then a whitetail buck spins and bounds through the trees, his white rump bristles, and his tail waves good-bye.

The chorus of ducks doesn't miss a beat, and we turn left at the lightning-scarred cottonwood toward Pond Lilly. A yellow leaf pirouettes out of the blue-black stillness through the white glare of my flashlight. Decomposing leaves cushion our footsteps and envelop us with the scent of decay. I shiver.

When I feel the slight rise of the levee, we stop. I turn off my light, and we wait for our eyes to adjust to the dark. Only then do we notice the gray of the eastern sky. Holding my Browning 12-gauge over-and-under in the crook of my arm, I feel for each step that brings me closer to our goal.

Pond Lilly, a fourteen-acre cornfield, is strategically located between Big Lake and the Illinois River. Shaped like an hour-glass, it rests in a slight depression three hundred yards west of the river.

Hunting Pond Lilly is a hit and miss proposition. Some years the river floods and prevents us from planting corn. Other years we plant, but the river drops so much that we can't get water to the field to flood it to give food to migratory flocks of mallards. And yet there are other years, rare years, years when the gods smile on us and everything goes right; we plant the corn, it grows, the river stays up, and just before duck season we flood the field so the ducks can find food.

Those years we hunt only every other morning to rest the field and give the ducks a chance to feed in peace. If you're a duck, feeding in Pond Lilly is sort of like playing Russian roulette. Most of the time it's quiet and safe, but if you fly in on the wrong morning you're gonna get the hell scared out of you.

Tom, John, Biz, and I line up behind willow bushes on the edge of the levee. Through the branches we can see black silhouettes of mallards on the edge of the corn splashing gray rings in the water. Cornstalks dance when ducks peck kernels off the ears.

I hear the metallic rasp of shotgun shells sliding into double-barrel chambers and the click of a safety.

"Let's wait until they leave, then hunt the doubles and singles that return." My companions nod.

"Yeah, but let's help 'em leave." Biz claps his hands.

The cacophony of sound is silenced by the specter of death. I hear Tom breathing.

In the middle of the field, a mallard explodes skyward through the cornstalks. Another explosion, another, another, and another. Singles, tens, hundreds, thousands of ducks roar into the sky, skimming the willows only feet over our heads. Fleeing bodies blot out morning gray, wingtips slice the air. My heart thumps wildly and I'm breathing as hard as if I'd experienced an orgasm.

"Wow!"

I can't tell who said it. Maybe they all did. Maybe I did. If I didn't, I should have. I glance at my two sons and my friend, their faces are turned upward in looks of awe.

When the last pair of mallards escape over our heads, silence descends on us.

"Wasn't that something?" Biz grins.

"Boy, I've never seen anything like that," John says.

"Not many people have experienced anything like that." I remember only one other time, hunting in Arkansas pin oaks.

"That was great, but where are we going to set up?" Tom asks.

"Impatient kid." Biz grins. "Just be sure you don't shoot a coot this time."

"Yeah, that was your fault, Biz. You told me to shoot." Tom's grin gets bigger. A first duck is a first duck, even if it is a coot.

"It'll be more fun to hunt together. If things get tough, we can split up," I suggest.

"Let's wade across to the blind with the open water in front. The ducks will land on it, if they come back," Biz said.

Small flights of mallards wing overhead, then flare, while we wade across the upper corner of Pond Lilly to a big blind camouflaged with cornstalks. A rising fireball glares at us through the trees to the east.

"Gonna be a clear day," Biz comments while we settle into the blind.

Tom sits on the far end of the bench, next to John.

"What's wrong, Tom? Don't want to sit between Biz and me?" I kid.

"You have to be careful of Dad and Biz," Tom tells John. "Last time we were here I sat between them. A flock of ducks decoyed, and those guys held me down so I couldn't shoot."

I laugh. "You still shot your limit, didn't you?"

"Us old guys need a head start." Biz grins.

"Here they come." I hunker down and wink at Biz. He nods as a pair of drakes flare out of the sun, swing high, and streak over the blind.

"Now!" Biz says. He and I remain seated to watch Tom and John jump up and blast at the mallards. Mortally wounded, one mallard locks its wings and sails to the far end of Pond Lilly, then splashes down. The other escapes low over the trees.

"Nice shot. Who got him?" I ask.

"Must've been John. I shot at the other one." Tom reloads. "Why didn't you guys shoot?"

"Wanted to give you young bucks a chance before we show you how to hit them." I laugh.

"We'll hit our share," Tom says.

"Sure you will. Well, I'll go get the duck to give you guys a better chance."

"I'll go with you, John. I hate to shoot ducks out from under the boys. Might get their limit for them." Biz laughs, and we slip into the water. Our boots sink into the muck. It's slow going through the corn rows.

Halfway across Pond Lilly, we hear a volley of shots. We turn but can't see over the cornstalks.

"Maybe they shot something," Biz ventures.

"I hope so, but I'm not holding my breath. They're still pretty green at this game," I say.

"Yeah, but they're safe and good sports." Biz breaths hard as he plows ahead of me. Too many cigarettes.

"We kid the boys a lot, but they're going to be good hunters." I push through the stalks to cut across to another row. I don't like to wade behind Biz with a loaded shotgun, even if it's broken open.

"When they learn to hit something." Biz points toward the shore next to a thick clump of willow bushes. "I think he fell over there."

There's another volley of shots from the blind. We still can't see if the boys hit anything. The ducks must be swinging in low.

"Ouch!" The rough edge of a cornstalk saws my cheek. I touch it and look at blood on my fingers.

It takes us about fifteen minutes to find the drake and during that time we hear more shots from the blind. Ducks fly overhead, and we know we've got plenty of hunting time left. We pick up the drake and head back toward the blind.

We hear whistling wingtips and look up to see a big flock of pintails swing past high above. The rising sun highlights their white bodies and dark necks.

"We're about 100 yards in front of you," Biz shouts to let the boys know not to shoot.

"Okay. We hear you and won't shoot." John's voice.

Several minutes later, we break out of the flooded corn rows to see Tom and John peering over the top of the blind at us.

Biz holds up the dead greenhead we found at the far end of Pond Lilly. "We got this one for you. Sorry you didn't hit any others."

"We had a great hunt. Shot our limit," Tom says and grins at his brother. They each hold up their limit of drakes in their right hand. Then they lift another bunch of ducks in their left hands.

"Dad, since you and Biz are such poor shots, we killed your limits, too! Hunt's over!"

"Jeeze," I mutter as we wade toward the blind. "Gotta teach the boys about sportsmanship and the law."

"Talk to them later, John. This only happens once or twice during a lifetime. Give them their moment of glory."

# OLE BLUE

Forty-five minutes before the sun explodes over the Flint Hills in Kansas, I stand, cased shotgun in hand, gloves on, coat collar pulled up, hat earflaps pulled down, shivering on the porch of the Cottage House in Council Grove. I wait for Dave, who is in his room attending to a last-minute detail.

Standing in front of me, Ole Blue, bathed in the pale wash of the thirty-watt porch bulb, coughs and shudders and sputters. Gray vapors spew out of its exhaust pipe and disappear in the night sky. I know those fumes will enlarge the ozone hole, and dismiss the thought of slathering my face with sunscreen. That idea's sorta like those irrational dreams you have just before waking.

I grin when I think of how Dave's other hunting partners describe Ole Blue to their wives. One might talk about its mileage, but four hundred thousand miles is not spectacular for a Suburban. Another would describe the myriad spots falling victim to rust, yet, in time, any vehicle that's exposed to the anti-ice salt spread by Midwest highway crews looks like Ole Blue. Someone else might talk about its arthritic doors, or the worn seat springs that give a unique butt massage.

"Let's go!" Dave, the ex-marine, commands, after kenneling Kate and Megan, two of his four English setters.

Hoping the heater works this year, I slide my shotgun in back, get in the passenger seat, and slam the door. It doesn't latch, so I slam it again, then give it a hard shove with my shoulder, to make sure it won't fly open on a curve. I won't fall out, but some of the floor litter might, and it could contain something valuable.

"Alan's trailering the rest of the dogs. He'll follow us with Rex," Dave says, referring to his quail-hunting brother and Rex Bosley, a retired surgeon from Boulder. Alan drives his new Jeep four-by-four and pulls their shiny eighteen-foot aluminum dog kennel. That rig's a hell of a contrast to Ole Blue.

Dave shifts into gear, and I breathe in deeply, savoring the best way to describe Ole Blue—its smell. The smell makes Ole Blue unique in the world of Suburbans; wet feathers, dog fart, Hoppe's Gun Solvent, vitamins, damp dog beds, bitter coffee, and fragments of cheese and other half-eaten protein snacks fallen between the seats. Buried somewhere in back under guns, boxes of shotgun shells, chains, jacks, tools, coolers, hunting coats, dog kennels, jugs of water, dog food, and one lost hunting boot, wafts the scent of yesterday's dead quail.

Doesn't get any better than this.

# MEMORIES OF THE
# HUNT

My first running cottontail with a bow. Shot while hunting with
Reid England. Canton, Illinois. 1962.

Dall sheep hunting, McKenzie Mountains, Northwest Territories.
The Northern Lights danced while the wolf looked like a ghost. 1976.

Central Illinois whitetail
taken from tree stand. 1971.

The morning before Nic Patrick and I
walked 15 miles back to the Wood
River, Wyoming, trailhead.  1992.

Bruce Creyke guided me to this 185 7/8 point Stone sheep
near Telegraph Creek, British Columbia. 1966.

Son Tom held for a perfect
heart shot on this bull elk.
Clarks Fork Valley,
Wyoming. 1995.

Son Tom shot this caribou several days before our crash landing, when he decided to marry Lori. Ellis River, Northwest Territories. 1989.

Jerry Mason measures Nic Patrick's bull caribou horns. Weymouth Inlet, Ungava Bay, Quebec, 1993.

In spite of a bouncing canoe and salt spray, George could spot a bull caribou miles away. Ungava Bay, Quebec. 1993.

Daughter Sue with elk rack
at Heinz Leuenberger's
high camp near Fernie,
British Columbia. 1973.

Curious bighorn lamb later untied my boot laces during bowhunt with Nic Patrick.
West Grinell Creek, Cody, Wyoming. 1991.

Woody Rumber shot this corn-fed whitetail in the early 1960s near Canton, Illinois.

The Pond Lilly Gang. Sons John and Tom, Biz Ford, and me with several greenheads. Central Illinois. 1970s.

Alaskan outfitter, Ken Oldham, examines the hind foot of an Alaskan brown bear. Cinder River, Akaska. 1962.

Outfitter Ken Oldham and Bill Neimi are dwarfed by Bill's Alaskan brown bear. Cinder River, Alaska. 1962.

# STRANGERS

Following his headlights east, Dave Hill fumbles for his cell phone and dials the message machine at his Boulder law office. Ole Blue crosses the Neosho River Bridge on the east side of town and begins to climb the long hill east while Dave dictates instructions to his secretary and leaves messages for his law partners.

Backwashed by a reddening sky, an immense statue of a spear-carrying Indian on horseback stands at the crest of the hill, a metal brave scouting for his past. I mouth a silent thanks to whatever artist shared his creative "gut sense" of history.

". . . and then we should . . ." Dave continues to give guidance for yet another legal deal. "I'll check with you between hunts and at noon, then . . ."

Looking out the window at the sunrise, I'm struck that Dave, even though he's a charge-by-the-hour attorney, is like all of us in today's world . . . time starved. We no longer have material poverty, we have time poverty. Time's our new currency; hours and minutes are more important than dollars and cents.

A new smell assaults me, and it forces me to trade off a cold right ear for fresh air when I lower my window.

Dave signs off his cell phone. "Might want to crack open your window."

"Already did."

"Oh." He glances at my window, then lowers his. "Must have an exhaust leak."

"Been like this for a while?" I ask.

"About a week. Got to get it checked." He turns left onto a gravel road and checks his rearview mirror to make sure his brother Alan follows us. Satisfied, he speeds up.

"We going to hunt one of your properties this morning?" I ask. Dave and Alan own a couple thousand acres of superb quail habitat, but they like to rest the coveys and have, over the years, developed relationships with local farmers. They now have permission to hunt on a lot of different places.

"No, we're going to hunt Mr. Brown's place. You remember that piece of land that runs along the river bottom."

"Oh." I remember two or three different places that are split by creeks and rivers, but I can't think which one is Mr. Brown's place.

"We'll stop at the next road, park Alan's rig and the dog trailer. You can wait there with Rex while Alan and I check in with Mr. Brown. He's pretty old and might not be comfortable with strangers."

I decide not to kid Dave about pulling up to Mr. Brown's with Alan's new four-by-four and shiny aluminum dog trailer. "How long have you and Alan hunted quail in this country?"

"We used to drive down here from Lawrence to hunt when we were kids. Been hunting here ever since. We know a lot of the folks here." Dave slows to look for a covey of quail that may have sought cover from hawks under a row of osage orange trees on the left side of the road.

The country turns into rolling grasslands, broken by timber, creeks, and, in the bottoms, earth scratched out of the timber for soybeans, wheat, sorghum, and corn. We drive past another abandoned farmhouse. Vines creep through its paneless windows, the branches of a tree reach through the collapsed roof. Its front door, once opened to greet neighbors and friends, lies on the front steps, rotting. This part of the country is littered with the corpses of dreams.

We haven't passed a car since leaving the highway. Dave turns left on a smaller gravel road and parks near the intersection. "You jump in Alan's car with Rex. We'll visit with Mr. Brown."

I sit in the driver's seat of Alan's new Jeep, savoring the smell of new leather and visiting with Rex. It's the first time we've hunted together.

In the rearview mirror, I see an old sedan approach. The car creeps past. Its driver, a woman, stares at us. I smile and wave. Frozen-faced, she doesn't wave back.

"Don't think she's happy to see us," I say.

"Probably just curious. You don't see many rigs like this out here." Rex watches her disappear around a curve in the road.

Four minutes later, having turned around, she approaches from the front and crawls past, intently studying us.

Thinking she might want to visit, I roll the window down. My wave doesn't alter her face. She speeds up, drives past us through the intersection, and about a mile behind us, near the crest of a hill, she turns left off the road toward a house and barn.

"Must have been looking out her window and seen us park here and gotten curious," I say.

"Probably doesn't see many strange cars out here. Especially something like the dog trailer," Rex says.

"Know how she feels, I've never seen anything like it either." I laugh, but feel uneasy. In my part of the world, someone would stop and ask what the hell's going on.

But this isn't my part of the world, and she didn't stop and ask. What's she doing now? Reporting drug dealers to the sheriff, or yelling at the old man, "Git yer shotgun! There's strangers about."

How can I think such paranoid thoughts on such a gorgeous morning?

"Here they come," Rex says.

I relax, swap seats with Alan, and tell Dave about the incident.

"Probably the tenant's wife. Curious."

"Talk with Mr. Brown?" I ask.

"Yeah. He's pretty old and seems to be bullied by his new tenant farmer, but he gave us permission."

Ten minutes later Dave pulls up to a barbed wire fence gate. "Get that for me. I'll pull up far enough to let Alan in."

While I wait for Dave and Alan to drive through the gate, I watch an old truck bounce over a hill in the pasture on the other side of the gravel road. It stops at the gate to their fence. A passenger in coveralls gets out, opens the gate. I'm happy to see they aren't hunters. The driver pulls through the gate and stops on the gravel road. He rolls his window down, hooks his elbow on the windowsill and stares at me.

"Morning!" I smile at them.

"All the quail in there's gotten old and sick and has died," the driver says in a loud voice.

"In time, that'll happen to us, too." I laugh and lift the loop over the gatepost to secure it, then hop in Ole Blue and am smothered by the smell of gas.

"Dave, that exhaust smell is terrible. Maybe we should check it," I say.

"We'll look at it when we park." He drives down a little-used tree-lined lane for about a half mile until it splits. A fallen tree blocks the path, but Alan swings onto the road to the right to park the dog trailer near a field.

Dave stops in front of the fallen tree, turns off the ignition and opens the hood. We're enveloped by gas fumes as we look at the greasy engine and carburetor and exhaust pipe fittings. Nothing looks out of place.

Rex walks up. "What's wrong?"

"We're getting exhaust fumes," Dave says.

Rex sticks his head under the hood with the authority of a surgeon. "I can't see anything wrong. Start the engine."

Dave turns the ignition, the engine coughs to life, then he joins us.

"There's the problem, there's a leak in the gas hose to the carburetor," I say, backing up. Little spurts of gas arch onto the hot engine block and vaporize into smoke.

Rex sticks his head under the hood and feels for the crack in the hose. I take another step back and hope Rex's best friend is a plastic surgeon.

"I'd better turn off the engine." Dave hurries back to the driver's seat.

During the next two minutes, Rex trims off the rotten gas hose and reinstalls it. It works fine.

"That tree's going to block the farmer. Let's move it for him," Dave says, opening Ole Blue's side door and digging through the stuff for a large box where he stores a long length of tow chain. We loop it around the tree and attach it to the hook under the front bumper. Dave puts Olde Blue into four-wheel-drive, throws it in reverse, and slowly drags the tree off the lane. He shuts the engine down and gets out to help us unhook the chain.

"What the . . ." We're startled by the sound of a racing engine and look up to watch a blue Ford pickup roar down on us. The driver slams on the brakes, swerving the truck into a skid that stops five feet short of Ole Blue's rear bumper. He flings open the door and leaps out screaming at us.

"What the hell do you dirty sons-of-bitches think you're do-ing coming on my property and leaving the gate open? Get the hell off now, or I'm going to—"

"Now just a minute, we—" Dave stands at Ole Blue's bumper and the guy runs at him, stopping just short of a fist in the face. Rex and I, standing by the fallen tree, look at each other.

"Don't 'just a minute me,' you dirty son-of-a-bitch. Get back in that Surburban and get the hell off my property . . . now!" The guy's jaw is twitching.

"Now, just calm down, friend. I know the owner of this prop-erty and—" Dave's voice, to a stranger, might seem cool and calm, but I can hear the tension in it. It's the first time I've seen Dave in this kind of situation, and I find myself watching him with an attitude of detached interest.

The guy cuts Dave off with another string of expletives and threats. Dave grows impatient with the foul language and his voice turns sharp.

"We have permission to hunt here from Mr. Brown."

"Like hell you do!" The guy yells, but there's an edge of un-certainty. It must have been Dave's use of the owner's name.

"Ask him!" Dave senses the change in the guy's voice, too.

"I don't have to ask him, I run the place for him, and—"

"Ask him! I just stopped up there and he gave us permission! We've hunted here for years. Drive up there and ask him!" Dave's using his old marine officer's voice.

"I will. And, by God, when I come back I'll have the sheriff and throw you bastards in jail." The guy turns toward his truck.

"You do that. Now go ask him!" Dave shouts at the guy's back.

We watch him jam his truck into reverse, spin around, and race back up the lane.

"Nice folks around here," I say, trying to ease the tension.

Alan walks up. "Who was that?"

"Must be the tenant for Mr. Brown," Dave says.

"I'll bet that was his wife who cruised past," I add as I put the chain back in its box.

Dave discusses the situation with Alan, then says, "We have permission. Let's go hunting."

When we gather at Ole Blue after the hunt the guy drives up again. This time he's calmed down and mutters something that could be taken as an apology, saying he was upset because he's been waiting all year to hunt trophy deer on the place and our dogs will run them out and ruin his hunt.

Dave wishes the guy the best of luck and waves as he drives back down the lane toward the gravel road.

We'd kicked up one six-point buck, a nice deer, but certainly not a trophy. There hadn't been the usual buck-in-rut scrapes and rubs that we see on other places. Maybe the guy's growing marijuana or something.

We hunt another place before driving to Eskridge for lunch. Its wide streets hold only a handful of old cars and pickups parked in front of the independent grocery store, the bank, and the cafe. Those stores not boarded up look like they can hold up for another few years, at least until the current aged generation dies off. Eskridge is a farm town that hasn't come to terms with its death.

Dave suggests that he and Rex eat in Ole Blue, while Alan and I eat at the cafe. Dave's concentrating on shedding pounds through a high-protein diet. Rex had a heart scare and is frightened to eat anything containing fat. They pack their own lunches. I'm a fanatic about having a wholesome meal, myself, like a double cheeseburger, fries, and apple pie a la mode. Heck, we'll burn off those calories during the afternoon hunt.

I talk them into bringing their lunches and joining us. "You can order something non-caloric to drink, and I'll leave a big tip so the waitress will be happy."

Conversations drop when we walk into the cafe, which is a decorated in Depression Nouveau. The place is crowded, and we ask a fellow in coveralls if we can join him at a long table that seats six. He nods. I wonder why he's the only one in the cafe who's eating alone.

Pretty quick, he reaches into his pocket and leaves five bucks on the table and mutters a good-bye. I see the amount written on his check and wonder why he left such a big tip if he didn't like the food.

People cast furtive glances our way, and I'm reminded of a scene from the movie *Deliverance*. The day's been sort of weird, or maybe my imagination is stuck in overdrive. I'm happy to leave Eskridge behind. It reminds me of my own mortality.

"We own the land to the south of the road, but you don't want to get caught hunting on the north side. The owner's mean." Dave parks Ole Blue in a dip in the gravel road. Alan pulls alongside and says he'll park on the road about a half mile ahead, so Dave and I can flush the quail toward them.

"If we don't, the birds'll fly to the north side of the road, and you know what that means." Alan says.

Dave and I flush a covey, which flies toward Alan's rig. Alan lets two of his setters out, and Megan and Kate join them to search for the birds.

The sun is low and casts a soft glow over the land, reddish and warm.

"Kate's on point!" I yell. I stand next to Alan, too far from the action, so we watch. Megan honors Kate's point, then Alan's two setters back. Dave and Rex, silhouetted against the sun's glow, move toward the four English setters that are framed rigid against the red sky. Rays of sunlight filter through Kate's tail feathering while she's locked rock-steady on the covey. The magic of that scene clicks into my memory bank to be pulled out and savored time and again in the future.

The quail explode into the air, Rex and Dave shoot doubles, and the dogs retrieve the birds. We pet the dogs, congratulate everyone for a fine day of quail hunting, and head back to Alan's Jeep, where he puts his dogs in their kennels.

"Why don't you stay here, John? I'll walk Kate and Megan back." Dave starts up the road toward Ole Blue, hidden from view in the dip in the gravel road.

Alan, Rex, and I reminisce about the classic beauty of the last shoot, then Alan says, "Dave'll be coming along in a minute, John. Rex and I'll head back to my rig.

I watch the Jeep and dog kennel disappear over the first dip, then I turn to the sound of tires crunching against gravel, expecting Ole Blue. It's not.

A black Dodge pickup crunches to a stop next to me. Its driver fills the seat, his jowls are heavy, eyes steel gray. He hooks his elbow over the windowsill, pokes his jaw at me and, with a nasty edge to his voice, asks, "What the hell you doing here?"

"Hunting," I say, fighting the impulse to point out the stupidity of his question. I'm standing in the middle of nowhere, with a

20-gauge Berretta over-and-under broken in the crook of my arm, and it's quail season.

"Which side of the road?" His eyes are ice cold.

"That side." I point, relieved. This must be the owner of the north side.

"You know who the hell owns that property?" He scowls.

"I . . . yeah, the Hill boys." The day seems to be circling back upon itself. I glance down the road at Alan's rig, disappearing over the horizon.

"Like hell! I own that property. What you doing hunting it?" The big guy's lips are tight.

My prayer that Ole Blue will crest the hill behind the guy's truck is unanswered. "Well, I'm sorry, I didn't know. See, I live in Wyoming . . . a guest of the Hills. I was told that it was their land." I'm desperate to weasel out of this. "I think . . ."

The big guy interrupts me with a laugh that turns into a guffaw. He sticks his maw out the window to shake hands. "I know that! Just talked to David up the road. He said you'd be here, waiting on him. Thought I'd kid you a little."

I miss his name when he introduces himself, but I catch the fact that he's a retired Air Force general.

He looks in his rearview mirror, then says, "Now, when David picks you up, tell him I shot a hell of a fine whitetail buck last hunting season down there where the line of trees crosses the creek . . . on their land."

"Yeah, I'll tell him." My throat is dry.

"You do that!" The general laughs, slaps my shoulder, and drives off, leaving me feeling like a stranger on that lonely Flint Hills road.

# INUIT WISDOM

"We'll take them to the killing fields and . . ." The Inuit guide stops speaking to two men of his village and watches me walk past their tent.

I nod at them, and remember reading about the killing fields of Cambodia. An image forms of the Inuits mowing us down in a barren Arctic place they call the killing fields as revenge for what whites did to destroy their way of life. I dismiss the fantasy.

These men of the Northwest Territories have Asian features, slight builds, dark complexions, black hair, and narrow eyes. They could be cousins of the Yi People I'd hiked with in 1989 through the Kingdom of Muli in the Szechwan Province of China.

One Inuit, wearing a hand-knit wool cap with a long tassel, sits on a wooden box next to the door of his canvas wall tent and fleshes out a caribou skin. The hide is spread, hair-side down, over his lap while he shaves the skin with his knife. He slices off a marble-sized fat glob, balances it on the blade, then picks it off with his lips and chews it like a ten-year-old with candy. He grins at me. Five or six of his teeth are missing.

I walk along a high bank and look for caribou crossing to this side of the Ellis River. It swirls its way toward the Arctic Ocean, five miles to the north. I wonder what they mean by "killing fields."

The next morning the guides board the six hunters in their twenty-foot aluminum boats, two hunters and guide per boat. We motor downstream from our camp to where the river dumps into the ocean. Three-foot waves churn the leaden gray Arctic. They check the wave action, then swing the boats east, open up their Yamaha 40-horsepower engines, and speed along the coast.

Son Tom and I huddle close together, backs to the wind and spray. Tom peeks out of his rain hood at the coast and points. "Caribou!"

George, our guide, slows the engine and glasses the animals. "Good bull!"

"You try for him, Dad." Tom shucks his rain jacket.

"The land's too barren, I'd never get close enough for a shot with my bow. You try."

"Okay." His fast response makes me happy.

The caribou drift over a ridge out of sight and George beaches the boat. The rocks scrunch under the weight of the aluminum bow, but the wind is in our face and I doubt if the caribou hear us. We leap out and drag the boat high on the beach.

I watch a boat containing my hunting buddy Jerry Mason and his partner, Jim Ricord, speed past. Jerry gives us a thumbs-up. I wave back. Their boat is closely followed by another boat containing Jerry's friend, Dave George, and his son-in-law, a Las Vegas detective. I hope Jerry, who shoots a .54-caliber muzzleloader, will be successful. He's at a big disadvantage against the rest of the hunters, who carry high-powered rifles.

We climb through the boulders to the top of the ridge and spot the white-maned caribou bull feeding behind the rest of the herd a hundred and fifty yards to the south. Tom lies prone, slams a cartridge into the chamber of his .30–06, thumbs off the safety, then aims, waits and waits for the bull to turn for a perfect broadside shot. He squeezes the trigger, and the bull crumples dead. I'm proud of his ability and patience to wait for the right shot.

An hour later, shouldering antlers, cape, and meat, we trudge back across the tundra toward our boat. The white sticks we are walking through come into the focus of my consciousness.

"Jeeze! Those are human bones." I point out a femur and fragment of a skull to Tom. George walks ahead of us, and I wonder if they're bleached bones of past hunters that had displeased him.

"Hey, George, wait up." Tom and I hurry to catch up with the short man whose Inuit name has been changed to "George" so clients can pronounce it.

George stops and waits.

"Are those human bones?" I point.

"Ancestors." His voice betrays no emotion.

"Ancestors?" I look at Tom, who studies another bone near his feet.

"When members of my village were too old to be useful, they paddled here to die." He doesn't smile.

"If they could paddle all this way, wouldn't they've been strong enough to have been of some use to the village?" I ask.

"Sometimes they had help paddling." George still doesn't smile.

"Oh." I watch Tom point to something half buried in the tundra.

"Is that what I think it is?" He looks at George.

George drops the meat, reaches down, picks it up, and hands it to me. "Keep it."

I turn the human lower jaw over in my hand and feel bad vibes. "Wouldn't it be bad spirits to take this away from here?" I ask.

"He doesn't care. Keep it." George gives us a rare smile.

I look at it and think that the missing teeth must be the result of too much raw caribou fat. I don't want to keep it. "I don't think . . ."

"Keep it." George picks up the meat and starts walking toward the boat.

I can drop the jawbone, but he might see it and interpret the gesture as disrespect. I know this Inuit man well enough to understand that he senses things I don't.

Feeling vulnerable in this strange place, I decide I'd rather piss off the dead than the living, so I stuff it in my backpack, pick up the caribou hide, and follow the distant relative of the Ancient One whose jaw now rests in my pack.

After lashing the caribou to the bottom, we launch the boat. George starts the engine and steers the same course as the other two boats. Rounding a curve ten minutes later, we beach next to the other boats and follow the rest of the hunters inland.

The killing fields turn out to be a vast barren plain along the coast where herds of musk ox congregate. Hundreds of musk ox, maybe a thousand, group in small herds. I wonder if they're family units.

After a half-mile hike, we stalk close to the herds. The hunters stand several hundred yards away from the musk ox. Each hunter picks out a large bull, then fires his scope-sighted high-powered rifle. I hear the bullets thunk into each animal's chest cavity. Leaning on my longbow, I'm a spectator to a scene I wish I were not witnessing.

In the distance, I spot movement and look through my 10x40 Lietz binoculars. Jerry is on his hands and knees, stalking through boulders, trying to get close to a bull. He wants to be under a hundred yards before he shoots his muzzleloader. The bull spots him, spooks, and trots out of range. I watch Jerry follow until he's out of sight. A short time later, we hear the distinctive *ka-boom* of his blackpowder rifle.

I listen for a second shot. It takes Jerry about a minute to reload, first pouring a powder charge down the barrel, placing a patched ball in the tip of the muzzle, then ramming it home tight with his ramrod. He then has to put an explosive cap on the nipple under the hammer, and finally he can shoot again.

Three minutes later there's still no second shot, so I know Jerry killed his bull with one shot. Good for him.

After the killing stops, I hear the sound of an engine, turn, and see one of the guides driving a large four-wheeler toward the carcasses where the hunters are getting their pictures taken.

"How'd you get that here?" I ask George.

"Brought it from Cambridge Bay in one of the boats. Makes hauling the meat back to the beach easier." He walks off to help load the meat onto the four-wheeler.

"You know, Dad, I think these Inuits have it figured out." Tom stands next to me.

"What do you mean?" I watch two Inuit guides cape one of the four toppled musk ox.

"I was talking to the cook last night. She said the men are responsible for supplying the village with meat for the winter. They've figured out that they can make money and lessen their work by charging hunters money to shoot their musk ox. The hunters get the horns and other parts the villagers can't eat, help with the work, and the Inuits get to keep the meat, which is what they wanted in the first place. It's a win-win for them."

"Yeah, makes a lot of sense," I say, but I still can't shake the emotional impact of the killings.

Two days later, it's my turn. Tom, as spotter, and I jump into George's boat and skim down the Ellis River to its mouth, punch into a choppy Arctic Ocean, and head down the coast to an area near the killing fields.

"Wind might rise," George mutters while we help pull the boat up on the beach. He carries the anchor to the end of its rope and digs it into the rocky beach to secure the boat from the twenty-foot tides.

An hour later, a violent gust of wind slams into us while we are climbing through a jumble of boulders separated by patches of grass. The ridge forms a seventy-five-foot-high hump that parallels the coast. Low clouds scud overhead, and we stop to watch the choppy sea turn vicious.

Standing helpless, a mile from our boat, we watch the ocean rise like a giant hand to seize our boat and drag it several hundred yards out, where waves swamp its gunnels. It sinks and settles on the shallow bottom. The outboard and bow of the boat bob in the rough seas. Oars and life jackets surface between white caps and drift toward shore.

"Shit happens," George mutters.

"How're we going to get back?" I pull my collar up against the bitter wind. We won't be missed until after dark, but it doesn't make much difference because the sea is too rough for a rescue. I imagine spending the night without a sleeping bag or tent on this barren Arctic tundra and hope the clouds don't bring freezing rain.

"Musk ox!" Tom points to the shoulder hump of a musk ox about a quarter of a mile away. Then we see the humps of other musk ox appear over the rocks. An entire herd is threading toward us downwind through the boulder field.

We squat behind a boulder, and I peer over the top to see the herd is scattered through the rocks feeding on the small clumps of grass. They don't see us.

"Look around side of the rock, not over top," George commands.

I slide down. Tom lies flat on his back between two boulders, so he won't spook the animals.

"Good bull coming." George points around the right side of the rock.

It's better than a good bull. His horns are massive. He's still a hundred yards away, but if he keeps on the same line, he'll pass within twenty yards, within bow and arrow distance. I drop out of sight, take an arrow out of my longbow quiver, and nock it on the string.

Their musky smell is carried to us by the wind. George puts his hand on my shoulder to stop me from peeking over the top of the boulder.

I hear grunts as the herd surrounds us. A cow passes ten yards to our left without noticing us. I'm spooked to realize we're going to be engulfed by a herd of musk ox, and I remember seeing videos of a threatened musk ox herd forming a crushing circle, horns outward. An image of us being in the center of that circle makes me want to laugh.

"He's close. Shoot now!" George whispers above the howl of the wind.

I raise my bow, too quickly. The herd spooks and thunders back the way they've come. I squat again, sick as I watch them disappear over the boulders.

"Too fast. Should have moved slow. Spooked them." George is full of wisdom.

"I was so excited . . ."

"Hide! They're coming back!" Tom falls to the ground and takes up his "I'm just another rock" position.

I can't believe it. The entire herd is feeding back toward us as if nothing had happened. "Why?" I ask George.

"Wind blows things. They stop and when they aren't chased, they think they're safe. Get down and don't get up until I tell you." George pushes me down to a kneeling position between the boulders.

We're scrunched tight together, my legs tangle with Tom's. I nock the arrow again.

"Closer. He's closer," George whispers.

"Where?" I'm blinded by the boulder.

"Same path." George inches to my right to give me room to rise and shoot.

My fingers grasp the bow string, and I try to pull my feet out from Tom's. George's hand is on my shoulder, holding me down.

"Slow your breathing!" George hisses in my ear.

I wondered where that panting was coming from. I gulp in big breaths of air to slow my breathing, but it feels as though I'll suffocate.

"Now, to your right! Slowly!" George grabs the back of my coat to prevent me from jumping up like last time.

I rise slowly, bow fully drawn. The bull is farther to my right than I expect and I twist to shoot. The arrow flies across the boulders and buries in the side of the musk ox, just back of the lungs and high. I think that I hit his spleen which will bring a sure death, but slow. I hate slow deaths.

We stand up to watch the bull rumble off with the herd, out of sight. On cue, my right leg begins to shake. Hyperventilating and a poor shot are bad enough. I shift my weight and lean against the boulder to hide the quaking limb from Tom and George.

We track the bull and finally find him, mortally wounded, but still alive, near the killing fields. I can't stand to watch an animal die slowly, so I borrow George's .243-caliber rifle and kill the bull.

There's a bitter taste in my mouth. I hate wounding an animal, even if I finally kill him. I remember the Inuit jaw in my pack and wonder if picking it up cursed me; first the boat sinks, then I screw up a shot and wound a magnificent bull musk ox. I skin the thick furry hide from the bull and am thankful that we'll have shelter to protect us from a long and bitter cold Arctic night.

As if reading my thoughts, George said, "We'll ride the four-by-four back to camp."

He finds the machine, straps the horns on the back, then Tom sits behind George on the seat. I sit on top of the musk-ox hide on the front platform and hold on as the four-wheeler grinds and bounces its way across tundra hummocks.

"It will be a long ride," George says in his classic understatement.

I think of the human jaw resting in my backpack and dismiss as superstition the thought that taking it from its resting place on the Arctic tundra could be a curse.

# MARRIAGE PROPOSAL

Thirteen minutes after turning north over the Arctic Ocean, the number four cylinder in the Otter's 450-horsepower radial engine explodes.

"Damn!" The pilot feathers the prop and pushes the yoke down to drop the plane's nose.

I watch the airspeed indicator. If we stall we die. The speed dips toward the red stall line, then regains the lost speed and holds steady.

The altimeter dips to fourteen hundred and fifty feet. We won't have much time. There's a light chop on the ocean surface below our pontoons. Thank God we're not in the midst of one of the frequent storms that rake this part of the world. Again I wonder if we're cursed by the jaw of the Ancient One that rests in my pack.

"Give me our latitude and longitude!" The pilot tosses the aeronautical sectional map at me. To get the best view from the co-pilot seat, I told him I'd logged over a thousand hours flying single-engine Bonanzas.

I grab the map and orient myself. The rocky Northwest Territory coastline is about twelve miles behind us. Too far to glide to safety. I see the mouth of the Ellis River on the eastern horizon.

"May Day! May Day! May Day!" The pilot screams into the microphone in his left hand. His right hand pushes the yoke down again to maintain our airspeed.

There's no response from the radio. The pilot drops the mike in his lap, switches hands on the yoke, and spins the radio dial to make sure he's on the aircraft emergency channel.

The Otter's loaded: son Tom and me, four other hunters, our sleeping bags, duffles, caribou and musk-ox hides, horns, gear from the camp, the pilot, and scrunched in the back on top of a pile of hides, the Inuit camp cook, who demanded to be flown back to Cambridge Bay instead of boating back across the Arctic Ocean with the guides. She's afraid of the water.

We don't have enough altitude to reach the coast, and it'll be tough to dead-stick the Otter onto a rough ocean surface; if we flip, most of us won't get out of the plane, but it won't make any difference—the water is so cold no one can last ten minutes.

I think about my son Tom dying in a watery Arctic grave. I'm flooded with self-anger. Why the hell did I bring him on this trip?

"Gimme the figures!" A sheen of sweat glistens on the pilot's forehead.

"I'm looking!" I find the mouth of the Ellis River on the map, follow the shoreline west, then note our position over the ocean. I follow the latitude lines to the edge of the map for the latitude number: 68 degrees, 11 minutes and 6 seconds. Then to the longitude line number.

I see a line that says "20 degrees E" and remember that depending where you are in the world, you have to adjust for true north. In the Midwest, where I'd flown, there was a very small range of adjustment. The closer you are to the North Pole, the more radical the adjustment. It's been years since I flew and I can't remember whether or not you adjust the longitude and latitude for magnetic variations. Broadcasting the wrong numbers would force search and rescue to look in the wrong place, a deadly mistake. If we survive the landing. I grab the pencil out of the pilot's shirt pocket and scribble the numbers on the map.

"The map says 104 degrees longitude, 68 degrees latitude. I've written them on the map, but they're unadjusted for true versus magnetic north. Check them out before broadcasting." I toss the map back in the pilot's lap.

He gives me a disgusted look, grabs his pencil, puts the map over the yoke, checks our location, then shouts into the mike again. "May Day! May Day! This is Otter CN-Nancy, Charlie, Alpha, Ralph. May Day! May Day!"

We listen; the radio is deadly silent.

I feel Tom's hand squeeze my shoulder, and I give him a thumbs-up, a lie. I look in back. Hunting buddy Jerry Mason's face is grim. His partner, Dave George, looks out the window, and I can't see his face. Behind them, two other hunters, the cop and Jim Ricord, stare straight ahead with unfocused eyes. The cop's fingers grip the edge of his seat. Sitting on a pile of caribou hides in the back, the Inuit cook's face is gray. She wrings the front of her coat in her hands.

"May Day! May Day! May Day! This is Otter CN-Nancy, Charlie, Alpha, Ralph. May Day! May Day!" The pilot's voice carries a sharper edge. No response.

The prop windmills. To our left, I see two tiny islands in the ocean, separated by a sheet of still water, a perfect landing place. I point and the pilot nods.

"That's gonna be it," he says. He jams the microphone back into its holder on the instrument panel, twists the yoke to the left, and dips the nose another couple degrees. The speed indicator shows he's holding it a hair above stall speed to get the optimum glide distance.

There's a retching noise, and I turn to watch the Inuit cook vomit. It spills over the front of her coat, the caribou hides. Yellow flecks splatter on the shoulder of the cop. He covers his face with his baseball cap.

I watch the two islands fill the Beaver's windshield, think again about the jawbone in my pack and understand why our plane was fated to crash. I've pissed off the Ancestors.

"I'm going to land between the islands and try to float to the beach," the pilot says.

"How can I help?" I'm happy he didn't use the word "try" with "land."

"There's a rope in the storage compartment on the pontoon. After we land, get it out, and if we get close enough to shore, jump off and pull us to shore," he says.

I try to remember the water temperature of the Arctic Ocean in September. I'd rather be flying so he'd have to jump into the frigid water to haul us to shore. On the other hand, my gear, with dry clothes, is in the plane.

Stop worrying, I tell myself, I probably won't have to get wet jumping off the pontoon because we'll die when we crash land, or crash water, or whatever.

I brace against a bar that runs down the side of the window as the pilot skims the Otter inches above the rocks on the larger first island. If we hit now, it's all over. He clears the first flat slab of rock and touches down on the water with a bump. We bounce once, twice, then settle in the water, and we cheer. Even the cook croaks out a cheer.

Now it's my turn. We're drifting toward the smaller island. I open the door and step down onto the wet pontoon, gingerly. I open the latch, find the rope, and tie it to a strut with three half-hitches. Holding onto the engine cowling for balance, I walk out to the end of the pontoon and wait for the plane to stop its movement.

I'm not about to jump into the water until the last minute. We drift closer to shore, yards become feet as the plane drifts closer to the beach. When it settles dead in the water, we're just a couple of feet from shore. I leap and get only one boot wet. Amazing. Maybe we beat the Ancestors' anger.

I pull the plane to shore, and smiling, everyone piles off.

"Help me carry this emergency radio to the height of land." The pilot hands me a two-foot square red box.

The island is about two hundred yards wide and five hundred long, its highest point is just four feet off the surface of the ocean. I help the pilot spread out long antennas across the ground.

"You did a hell of a job handling that plane. Ever made an emergency landing before?" I ask.

"Yeah, three times." He opens the lid to the box that contains the radio.

"Oh?" I ask.

"This year," he says.

I don't want to know how many times he'd pulled off crash landings before this year.

He holds the microphone close to his lips and cries, "May Day! May Day! This is Otter CN-Nancy, Charlie, Alpha, Ralph. May Day! May Day!"

The emergency radio is as silent as the radio in the Otter. Tom looks worried, so I suggest that we stretch our legs. We walk along the shore toward the end of the island.

"Were you scared, Dad?" Tom asks.

"Hell, yes. Weren't you?" I put my arm around his shoulder and squeeze.

"Yes, I was scared. What were you thinking about, Dad. You know, up there?"

"Irrational thoughts. Nothing like my life flashing before my eyes. I was afraid that you'd die."

"Oh." He swings his arm around my waist and gives me a hug.

"What were you thinking about?" I ask.

"Sorta puts things into perspective. I was thinking about what's important to me."

"Like what?" I ask, as we approach the end of the island. Twenty feet away, there's an old four-by-eight-foot piece of plywood wedged upright between boulders. A small hole had been cut out of its middle; a blind for an Inuit seal hunter.

"Think we'll get off this place?" He doesn't ask if we will die here.

"Sure. When we don't show up, they'll send out a search plane." I look at the sky for an approaching storm. The overcast is solid, but it doesn't look like a storm.

"So, we'll stay here for a while?" He looks at me.

"More than likely, but that's no problem. We have our sleeping bags and other gear on the plane. Maybe there's some meat, but I think the guides are bringing all the meat back to Cambridge Bay in their boats." I don't mention that we don't have any water to drink, other than what might be on the plane.

"Yeah." He looks thoughtful.

"So what's important in your life?" I ask.

"I decided I'm in love with Lori. If we get off this rock, I want to marry her." He gives me an embarrassed grin.

"That's wonderful." I'm chagrined I hadn't thought about Tish or the other kids.

We stand next to the plywood blind, silent for a moment.

"Really think we'll get out of here?" he asks again.

"Sure. One way or another," I say with as much confidence as I can muster.

"Gotta pen?"

"Nope. Just the felt-tip I used to mark our address on my bow case for the airline." I feel for it in my shirt pocket.

"That'll do." He holds his hand out for the marker and I watch him write on the plywood.

> Lori—if I die here, I want you to know
> I love you with all my heart.
>
> Love, Tom

I choke up and use the back of my glove to wipe tears from my eyes. He hands me the marker, and we walk back to huddle with Jerry and the other hunters and wait.

Six or seven hours later, we hear the sound of a motor, but it's not a plane. It's the roar of an outboard engine, bringing the first of our guides to the island. It's a miracle. We learn they use the shelter of the islands on their way back across open water to Cambridge Bay. Now, if we have to, we can ride back to Cambridge Bay with them across the open Arctic Ocean.

The radio remains silent, but two hours before dark a twin-engine Otter, outfitted for short-field landings and takeoffs, swoops over, swings a wide circle, makes three passes at the larger island, then lands and bounces to a stop.

The guides ferry our pilot across to confab with the pilot of the twin Otter, then he returns and we gather around him.

"He can only take three of you and your gear at a time. Who's going first?"

I interpret the silence of the group as reluctance to show how anxious everyone is to get off this barren little rock in the Arctic Ocean. The Inuit cook looks at the boats, then the twin Otter waiting on the far island and says, "I go in boat now."

"You guys go ahead. Tom and I'll wait," I say, hoping that our companions don't suspect my reason for waiting. Takeoff requires more runway than landing. I'm not sure the pilot can lift the twin Otter off before running out of island and I'm not about to risk Tom's life twice in one day. On the other hand, Tom and I've been at risk ever since George insisted I keep the jaw of the Ancient One. It's time to break the curse.

Our pilot packs up his emergency radio and antennas, while everyone separates their gear and loads it in the guide boats. When the guides ferry the first group to where the evacuation Otter awaits, I mosey to the middle of our island, remove the Ancient One's jaw from my pack, and place it on the ground, sheltered between two rocks.

"Rest in peace, old timer . . . and leave us alone." I turn and join Tom on the shore to hear the Otter's twin engines rev to a roar, then watch it bounce across the rock rubble, slowly at first, then gaining speed until, at the water's edge, the pilot jams down the flaps and the plane shutters off and skims the waves. We watch the plane climb, then bank left toward Cambridge Bay. I wish we were on it. I hope weather doesn't close in. I hope he comes back for us.

At dusk, we hear the twin Otter's engines, and George, our guide, ferries us across to the other island. We shake hands and I resist telling him I left the Ancient One's jaw on the island.

Soon we're airborne again. This time I sit next to Tom, and when we see the lights of the airport in Cambridge Bay I ask him, "Gonna change your mind?"

"What do you mean?" His face is pressed against the window, looking at civilization.

"About marrying Lori?"

He turns from the window and a slow grin spreads across his face. "Heck, no!"

"Good. She's a fine woman." I'm sorry I didn't have a saw to cut out his words on that piece of plywood. It would have made a heck of a conversation piece in their old age.

# SOUL MUSIC

The bow of the twenty-five-foot-long canoe chops through Ungava Bay's waves, which spray heavily against our backs. Willie, our guide, says, "Wind rising. We go back now." He nods to the fat kid in the stern of the canoe, who gooses the 40-horsepower Yamaha outboard motor.

"Pretty slow hunting." Tom is discouraged. We haven't seen many bull caribou.

"We've got four days of hunting left. Maybe we'll spot a good one on the way back to camp," I say and look at the barren landscape.

Northeast of Quebec's Hudson Bay, Ungava Bay lies next to Newfoundland and the Labrador Sea. Its northern neighbor, Baffin Island, is cut by the Arctic Circle. One of the hunters says the camp is sub-Arctic, but the land, water, and sky make it feel like it's above the Arctic Circle. So do the native people.

Tom looks at his watch. "Don't have a lot of time before dark."

"We've still got time for a short hunt," I say.

I sit next to Tom, back to the bow, and watch for caribou on the land between the fjords. I tighten the drawstings on the hood of the heavy rain suit, then tuck the fletching of my arrows under my arm so they don't get soaked. Cold water sloshes against our rubber boots in the bottom of the canoe.

We weave along the rocky shore, then find calmer water where Fat Kid cranks open the throttle.

"There's a good bull!" Tom points.

I see antlers and the white ass of a caribou disappear over a ridge.

"You try?" Willie asks.

"Yeah. A quick stalk," I say.

Willie motions to Fat Kid, whose normally impassive face frowns when he turns the canoe toward shore.

"It's your turn, Dad."

I shuck the rain suit and stow it under the metal brace in the corner of the seat just as the bow crunches against the pebbles on the shore.

Willie jumps out and says to Fat Kid, "Not long. You stay here with boat."

Fat Kid looks past the point of land at the heavy seas, then nods.

I notice Tom and Willie keep their rain suits on, but they don't have to get close to the bull. The noise of the suit would alert a caribou.

We walk up the ridge under a leaden sky and into a strong wind.

"Was the bull spooked?" I ask.

"Think he was feeding into the wind," Tom says.

Willie drops to his knees near the top and peers over. "He goes over next ridge."

We follow for a half hour.

"We don't catch him. Too fast. Time to go," Willie says.

I look at the sky and feel a raindrop when we crest the ridge next to the beach.

"Where's the boat?" I ask Willie.

He shrugs. "Maybe in next cove."

We walk to the next cove. Empty.

The next cove. Empty.

"Maybe he go around point. Wait on other side," Willie says, turning inland.

We walk toward the other side and pass a rocky ledge that runs down to the water. I notice a thirty-foot-long, two-foot-high overhang where the ledge meets the sloping ground just above the high-water mark.

Raindrops split the dusk and I regret leaving my rain suit in the canoe. I think about the two times I've had hypothermia and shudder.

We climb around a thirty-foot cliff to reach the far shore and find nothing. We use our binoculars but can't see Fat Kid.

"Where do you think he is, Willie?" Tom asks.

"Hope he's okay," Willie says, scanning the whitecapped waves beyond the point of land.

I'm not concerned about Fat Kid at this point; we can't help him. He's got the boat and my rain suit.

"What're we going to do, Willie?" I ask.

"Maybe wait for him. Maybe walk back," he says.

The ground is a combination of rocky ridges, cliffs, and bare tundra. There are no landmarks. No stars. The rain is heavier.

"How long will it take us to walk back to camp?" I ask.

Willie shrugs. "Not sure."

"We're not going to crash around all night in a rain storm trying to find camp. Follow me," I order, pulling my head lamp out of my pack.

A half hour later, I find the crack in the ledge. "We're spending the night here. It's too dangerous to try to find camp. I don't have a rain suit, and it's starting to pour. Find yourself a dry spot."

"No wood for a fire," Tom observes.

I lie down next to the crack and roll in. It's just wide enough to keep me dry if I lie on my back, but if I curl up, either my butt or knees will be under the drip line.

"Home away from home." Tom laughs as he crawls in just above me. I'm not worried about him. He spent a couple months at the National Outdoor Leadership School, camping in snow caves during Yellowstone's winter. He's tough and knowledgeable.

"Do you miss Lori?" I ask about his wife.

"Sure, but I'm glad she doesn't know about this," he says.

Willie squeezes in below me and moves a flat rock under his head for a pillow. He's done this before. Then he shines his flashlight toward the sea. Rain streaks through its yellow beacon.

I rest my head on my pack.

"Sorry, but I don't have much room. I've gotta put my leg over your shoulder," Tom says.

We listen to the waves hammer the shore, the moan of the wind, and the rhythmic drip of water falling from the ledge . . . sad soul music.

About an hour later, I ask, "Willie, when do you think the other guides will search for us?"

"They won't," he says, still shining his beacon light to sea.

"Why not?" Tom asks.

"Because I'm head guide, and if I'm not there to tell them what to do . . . " he trails off.

"Well, if they're not coming, why are you wasting your batteries by shining your flashlight out to sea?" I ask.

"Make you feel better," Willie says.

Tom and I laugh. "Well, turn the darned thing off and get some sleep."

"Okay." Willie adjusts the rock under his neck, and within seconds I hear his soft snoring.

I get cold, then remember the emergency foil blanket in my pack and struggle to get it out, unfold it, and cover my body. It feels pretty flimsy. Although I've carried one for years, I've never had to use it.

"You okay, Dad?"

"Yeah, just a little cold. Put my emergency blanket on. I'll be okay."

"Good," Tom says.

A few minutes later, I listen to both of their snores. The blanket is holding some of my body heat.

I wake in the middle of the night. "Hey, Tom."

"Huh?"

"My hands are freezing. Can I put them between your legs to warm up?"

"Sure." He begins snoring again.

A short time later, I feel Tom shift and, through his sleep, he mutters, "Oh, Lori!"

I jerk my hands from his thighs and laugh.

Later, he wakes up. "You awake, Dad?"

"Yeah. Cold."

"Me, too," he says.

Willie continues snoring. I put my hand out. "Feels like it's stopped raining."

"Let's get out and warm up," Tom says.

"Can't build a fire."

"Come on. We'll do jumping jacks." Tom rolls from under our little ledge, and I join him.

We turn on our headlamps so we don't stumble and do a series of jumping jacks, then do step-ups on a flat, two-foot-high rock until our blood circulates and we feel warm. Willie's snoring stops. I know he's watching, and I laugh out loud, wondering what he thinks about his crazy hunters.

We start walking as soon as we can see and four hours later walk into camp. Our hunting companions, Nic Patrick and Jerry Mason, tell us they fired a rifle throughout the night, hoping the sound would guide us to the warmth of our tents.

We gather in the dining shack where the cook fixes us hot oatmeal, pancakes, bacon, and toast.

"Did Fat Kid drown last night, Willie?"

"No. He come back here." Willie shovels a spoonful of hot oatmeal into his mouth.

"Why'd he leave us stranded?" I ask.

"He miss his boom-box and want to hear his MTV music," Willie says.

Fat Kid listened to his MTV music, while we listened to the soul music of wind and rain and waves.

# ROCKY MOUNTAIN
# OYSTERS

The Canada geese flew back to their resting areas by mid-morning, so I suggest to my hunting buddy, Fred Ayers, and our guide, Tom Bruno, that we have an early lunch before the afternoon hunt.

Tom heaves his six-foot-five, two-hundred-ninety-pound hulk out of the pit, then reaches down and gives Fred, who stands five-nine, a hand.

"You boys ever been to Bruce's Bar in Severance?" Tom asks, as we walk through the decoys toward the truck.

"Nope. What's the attraction?" I ask.

"Bruce's claims they serve more fried Rocky Mountain oysters than anyplace in the country," Tom says.

"God, I haven't had a plate full of oysters since I was a kid. My granddaddy used to cook up a batch every spring, right after he castrated the calves." Fred grew up hunting and fishing in the tidewater country of Virginia.

I remain silent, unwilling to share the fact that I've never eaten Rocky Mountain oysters.

Severance, Colorado, has seen better days. I hit the brakes to swerve around a mongrel who is sleeping in the middle of the road. Severance consists of a couple worn-down buildings, a few homes, several trailers, a gas station on the corner, and its claim to fame, Bruce's Bar.

Bruce's is a white-washed concrete block building that sprawls a half a block or more. A painting of a huge bull standing on tip-toes, front hooves between its legs and a grimace on its face, dom-inates the east wall of the building. Painted under the picture of the bull is a proud statement that Bruce's served more Rocky Moun-tain oysters than anyplace in the country. Just like Tom said.

We walk into the dim, smoky interior. A low wooden ceiling presses down. Four old guys hunch over the bar. One turns on his stool to glance at us, then turns back to the company of his Bud-weiser. The scene doesn't do much for my appetite.

We select a table close to the bar. When my eyes adjust to the light, I see another hundred or so empty tables and an old juke-box on the far side of a small dance floor. I imagine what the place would be like on a Saturday night.

A waitress waddles over. She has a pencil stuck in her gray bouffant hairdo, and her face looks sweet and grandmotherly. An apron covers her belly. I can't tell if it's the dim light, or just a dirty apron.

"So what'd ya want, boys?" She pulls an order pad from her apron pocket, takes the pencil out of her hair, licks its point, and holds it an inch above the pad.

Tom grins. "I'll have a plate of oysters and coffee."

I was hoping he'd order a cheeseburger. Now it's up to Fred.

She turns washed-out eyes on him. "How about you, sweetie?"

Fred slides the worn menu between the bottle of catsup and the salt and pepper shakers. "I'll have the same."

My hope for a graceful way out crashes with his order.

The old gal looks at me and smiles. "And you?"

"Huh . . ." I squint at the menu.

"You've had Rocky Mountain oysters before, haven't you?" Fred asks. There's a little incredulous dance to his voice.

His question demands a "yes" or "no" answer. I'm caught.

I look at the waitress. "Huh . . . how do you cook them here?"

She glances at my menu. I know what she's thinking. The top of the menu screams, in huge bold letters, "Fried Rocky Mountain Oysters."

I decide confession would be good for my soul. I give grandmother a pleading look. "I've never had Rocky Mountain Oysters before. Think I'd like them?"

I'd like to take back my words, but it's too late.

She gets a little smirk on her lips. "Do you like frankfurters?"

"Huh?" My hearing gets bad when I get nervous.

"Do you like hot dogs?" Her smirk turns into the beginnings of a smile.

"Oh . . . Yeah, I really like hot dogs!" I try to ignore the look on Fred's face.

She cocks her head and a huge grin spreads her lips. "Well honey, hot dogs are made with lips and assholes. If you like hot dogs, you'll love the nuts!"

# EULOGY FOR A BEAR

It's a weird time. The summer and early fall of 1988 is unlike any other for the past 400 years; since the last awful conflagration. Yellowstone is burning.

The fires start in June and we wait. It's like watching a loved one die of terminal cancer, slow and agonizing.

Our place is downwind of the flames. We pray it won't hit the Clarks Fork Valley, but in rare objective moments that summer, we know the fire will come.

The air is filled with smoke. Choking, waiting, listening to rumors, knowing that your dream place might turn to ashes makes rational thought a struggle. Other thoughts get out of perspective, too.

One of my twisted thoughts is that if the cabin burns down, we can rebuild, but I can never replace a lost hunting season.

When I realize that I have more hunting seasons behind me than ahead, the noxious fumes of depression penetrate my mind.

We do what we can to prepare for the worst if the fires hit. I drive with my neighbor, Mike Evans, to Billings and buy the necessary equipment to build a fire truck: a 500-gallon water tank, pipe, a Jacuzzi pump, 600 feet of fire hose, and two nozzles.

Another neighbor, Rick Wogoman, lends me his 1948 Dodge flatbed truck, on which I mount the tank, pump, and hose.

Our summer's life of denial is continually interrupted by reminders of what could come. The smoke, drifting from fires sixty miles to the west, is so thick we develop coughs. The river, usually wide and blue, slows to a trickle. Sunlight filters through forty thousand feet of smoke to color the water a dull copper.

One day, the prevailing winds shift and the sky clears. My wife Tish and I sit on our deck, drink iced tea, and look at the blue sky above. Something falls from the sky.

"What's that?" Tish asks.

I pick it off the deck and examine it. "It's a burned twig."

"A twig?"

I show it to her and say, "That's the damnedest thing I've ever seen. It must have been pushed up to the jet stream by a column of smoke."

Just then another drops, then another. Charred twigs, about half the diameter of my little finger, are falling from the sky.

I look at the blue sky. "The jet stream must be carrying them."

Bathed in sunshine, we watch charred debris from the fire fall for an hour.

Suddenly, I think of something that happened that spring up in the wilderness area. I had spotted the tracks of a huge black bear. They reminded me of the other bears I hunted, Alaskan browns and mountain grizzlies. When I studied this bear's tracks, I knew I wanted to hunt for him.

When news comes that the fires hopped into the North Crandall drainage, our kids, John, Tom, Sue, and her husband, Tim, come up to help. They skinned the logs to build our cabin.

We nail sheets of plywood over our picture windows, and I spike Rainbird lawn sprinklers on the ridgelines of our shake-shingle roof. I turn on the water and let it run day and night to soak our cabin.

A neighbor stops by to tell us the latest rumor. He looks at the sprinklers on my roof and asks, "How long you plan to run those?"

"Until the fire comes through."

He takes off his Stetson and wipes sweat from his forehead with the back of his wrist. "Run them that long, you're going to burn up the motor in your well."

"Yeah, probably. Doesn't make much difference, does it?" I look at the smoky sky.

Winds caused by the fire spike high and sparks fly over the ridge into the Pilot Creek Valley. That night we pile into our trucks and drive up to the Beartooth Highway overlook of Pilot Peak.

"Wow! Looks like Christmas lights on a gigantic tree," Sue says.

"Looks more like when you're in a jet flying into Manhattan," counters John.

Tom, our younger son, who spent the last several summers building buck-and-rail fence and corrals, remains silent. He has a lot of emotion wrapped up in the place.

Even though the wind shifts and the spot fires in Pilot Creek die down, we decide it's time to evacuate our good stuff from the ranch, so we load the horse trailer and drive it to a storage unit in Cody, a seventy-mile, kidney-jarring trip over unpaved Dead Indian Pass.

One morning the government moves sixteen hundred firefighters and National Guardsmen into the valley. They set up camp in a big meadow near the confluence of Crandall Creek and the Clarks Fork River. They put up tents, make streets, put up street signs, build a post office and movie theater, all in a couple days.

Several days later, the troops get restless waiting for the fire. The camp commander orders them to tear down and reset their tents in straighter lines.

My family gets restless, waiting, waiting for the flames. I need to give them something to do to keep them occupied.

The year before, I planted wildflowers. The mix contained the seeds of what I call beggar's lice. The damned little burrs stick to the dog, to our shoe laces, our pants, our shirts, and even to the hair on our arms.

Like the fire camp commander, I order my troops to seek out and pull up the beggar's lice plants. Unlike the camp commander, after an hour or so, my troops rebel. Nasty words and phrases fly my way. I'm lucky I'm not lynched.

We've done about everything there is to do. Now we can only wait.

The inside of the cabin is dark and, except for our beds, without furniture. We sit on the floor. We don't have TV, and radio reception is poor. However, we do have a radio scanner, and we listen to a hotshot fire crew getting trapped above the limestone rim near Squaw Creek. We hear panic rise in their voices while they try to outrun the flames. Just in time, a local gets on the radio and guides them to an elk trail off the limestone rim and into the valley and safety.

Tish and I lie in bed watching the reddish glow of the fire over the ridge across the river. A pine on top of the ridge explodes into flames. The clock says 1:10 A.M.

Tish turns to me. "I guess this is it."

Later, our phone rings.

"Hello?" I answer.

"Mr. Winsor?" a woman's voice asks.

"Yeah?"

"There's someone at your door." She sounds irritated.

"Huh?"

"Please go to your front door. Mac Black is there." Mac's our local game warden.

I stumble down to the door, and there stands Mac. The red lights on his rig are flashing. "Fire's over the top. It's time to go, John."

"Go where?"

"Evacuate." A sardonic little smile plays on Mac's lips. I can't figure out if it's caused by nerves or the sight of me wrapped in a towel.

"Gotta pack my office and haul the horses to the Salanger place," I say.

"Game and Fish is tracking seven radio-collared grizzlies down there. Probably pushed out of the park by the fires. If there are seven with collars, there are more. Be careful."

I go back up to our bedroom and stand next to the open double doors. As I watch more trees explode high on the ridge, I decide we have plenty of time. I go back to bed and sleep soundly, in a sense relieved that the damned fire is finally here.

At dawn, we gather the horses from the upper pasture. They gallop into the corral, kicking and bucking and snorting. We catch and halter each one. Their eyes are wide and wild, their nostrils flare, but they get into the trailer without trouble. Maybe they understand it's time to leave.

Tom hauls them twenty-three miles down to Sunlight Basin, then twelve more miles up the Sunlight dirt road to the Salanger place. An old homestead split by Sunlight Creek, it has pastures dotted with thick clumps of willows and is hemmed in by high cliffs on both sides. Any bear coming from the park passes through there. Tom and I agree we won't be upset if the bears take one of the horses. The grizzlies don't have much else to eat.

Tom returns just as a group of hard-hatted, yellow-shirted firefighters pull in. The camp commander minces no words. "Get the hell out of here. Now!"

I show a young firefighter my fire truck, then jump into my pickup.

"Hey! Hey!" he shouts and runs after me. I stop and lean out the window. "Where are the keys?" he asks.

I laugh. "That truck doesn't need a key. The starter is on the floor."

"Oh . . ." He returns to my fire truck. His uncertainty makes me stay and watch him. Sure enough, he can't figure it out. I mumble something about the younger generation, get out, and show him how to start it.

We drive down the valley toward Cody. Thick smoke turns the middle of the afternoon into midnight. Grass and sagebrush flame on each side of the road. Trees explode. We're disoriented. It's like wandering through Purgatory.

We bunk out at the Holiday Inn in Cody. Sometime after midnight, my buddy Nic Patrick calls. "Marshall Dominick at the 7-D just called. The fire's breached the ridge into Little Sunlight."

"I can't believe it," I say. "That fire ran twenty-three miles in just a few hours."

"We'd better get your horses off of the Salanger place." Nic volunteers to take Tom back to get them and haul them to his ranch in Cody.

The next morning Tom returns. "You can't imagine how scary it was up there. We didn't have flashlights but found a couple of Coleman gas lanterns in the old cabin. So there we were, walking around through those thick, bear-infested willows, looking for the danged horses. They were spooked by the glow of our lanterns through the smoke. They ran off through the brush, then we'd hear something charging behind us. We'd spin around to see a pair of eyes staring at us. We didn't know if it was a horse or a grizzly bear."

We turn on the TV. Newscasters are talking about yesterday as "Black Friday." There's nothing more the kids can do, so they return to their homes in Colorado and their own lives.

Later that morning Tish and I talk our way past the guards at the roadblocks and drive back over Dead Indian Pass. We're quiet, struggling with our own emotions and fears of what we'll find.

Smoke hugs the treetops. Our nostrils fill with the stink of charred earth. Near Crandall Creek, we spot a neighbor leaning against his pickup along the side of the road. He works at the fire camp. He tells us a firefighter had told him that they'd saved all but one building in the valley.

"Mrs. Cary's store burned to the ground. Now, ain't that what you'd call poetic justice? That camp commander begged her to stop selling whisky to his Indian hotshot crews. She told him to go to hell . . . it's a free country and she'd sell anything she wanted to anyone she wanted. A fireball slammed on top of her roof. Nobody came to help.

"Well, they saved a bunch of cabins and worked at public relations. Should'a seen them run when the fire swept through their camp. That's the gum-ment for you."

"What happened to that big bull elk that hung around the fire camp?" Tish asks.

"Don't know. Haven't seen him since the fire came through. Probably burned up."

We wish our neighbor good luck, then drive toward our place.

"I've never heard the term 'gum-ment' before. What's he mean by that?" Tish asks.

"I don't know for sure, but from the sound of his voice I think it means 'enemy of the people.'"

Driving through five miles of charred landscape, I turn off the road and drive through our gate. Our upper pasture didn't burn. I'm hopeful until I see the trees on the rock knob above the cabin. They look like black skeletons, their smoking limbs pleading to God for rain. The bile rising in my throat is as acrid as smoke from the fire.

When I drive down the hill from the upper pasture, I'm relieved to see that the trees along the river and around the barn haven't burned. I'm filled with hope for our cabin.

The east knob of the hillside across the river is smoldering black, yet just to the west, the timber is still green. However, tendrils of smoke curling through the trees show it'll be just a matter of time before it burns.

I drive through the strip of green timber between the barn and the cabin and enter a war zone. Everything but our cabin is charred black and smoking. I stop the truck, and we watch a tree that escaped the initial burn explode into flames. A few minutes later, it joins its smoldering brethren. I'm consumed, too, with a feeling of helplessness and hate.

Tish, forever the optimist, says, "Look, our cabin didn't burn."

We stand on our porch and survey the damage. Our cabin and everything south toward the river and to the east is untouched. Everything west and north is burned crisp; thousands of lodgepole pine and grasses. An acrid stench fills the air.

"Look." I point to the new buck-and-rail fence Tom built. Several sections still stand, many are burning, most are straight white ashes against the blackened earth.

Tish looks sad. "He worked so hard to build it."

The remains of flares indicate that the firefighters had started a backfire at the edge of our porch. Then, when the leading edge of the flames reached the timber on the north side of our cabin, the wind must have shifted because the fire turned and climbed the two-hundred-foot cliff that separates us from the upper pasture.

Nothing I can do will save our view to the west, so I go to work on the hillside across the river where spot fires threaten to spread and create another inferno.

Smoke hisses into my face when the thin stream of water pumped from my rubberized backpack hits burning embers. I cough and spit into the black ashes of the fire. My spittle scatters gray-black ashes.

My feet are scorched from walking in hot embers buried under inch-thick ashes. My leather hunting boots are now cracked and curled. I'll have to buy another pair before next hunting season. Next season, I think—this one is shot. I mourn the loss of the hunting season as I mourn the loss of the burnt land.

I empty my water-pump, then shovel dead pine needles away from a burning tree stump. My feet kick up clouds of ash when I walk over to lean against an unburned tree. Its trunk, so large I can't put my arms around it, is hot against my back. Its bark is hot to the touch. I hear a roaring noise and put my ear against its rough bark. The roaring is inside the trunk. Walking around the tree, I see that a wind-blown ember had wedged in the crotch of the roots. The wind acted like a blacksmith's bellows. The ember's flames bored inside the tree and hollowed it out from the inside. Invisible, it burns up the core of the tree.

I step back and see the pine that soars into the smoke-filled sky in a new light. It looks healthy, in its prime, yet its insides are being eaten alive. It's the same way my father died, eaten alive by cancer, slowly.

I'm consumed by sadness. Sadness for my dead father, for this dying tree, and for my loss of both of them. I take off my gloves and wipe tears away. I sigh and stare across the river valley at my cabin, then I pick up my shovel and turn toward the smoldering hillside.

There is a movement on a ridge several hundred yards to the east. An immense black bear is slowly picking its way through the trees toward the river. I wonder if it is the one that had made the tracks in the wilderness area last spring.

The bear stops, sniffs the ground, takes one step forward, then sniffs the ground, takes another step. When he smells hot embers in the under-matting of the forest floor, he backs up and tries another direction.

It has to be the bear I wanted to hunt. Filled with renewed energy, I drop my shovel, crouch low, and work toward a ravine that cuts toward the river. Out of sight in the ravine, I sprint downward, jump over fallen logs, and slide down the steep hill on my butt. I splash through the shallow river and scramble up the far bank, then sprint to the cabin for my longbow. I string the bow and trot down the drive toward the barn. My intent is to turn right on the path that leads from the barn toward the river, then wait on the bank for the bear.

The bear surprises me by stepping out of the forest seventeen yards in front of me. He stops in the middle of the gravel drive and watches me fumble a broadhead from my bow quiver. He's even bigger than I imagined. My fingers nock the arrow onto the string and slowly raise the bow. Pulling the arrow back until I feel the back of the razor-sharp broadhead cut against the forefinger of my left hand, I smell the copper scent of my own blood.

The bear stands perfectly still, his broad head turns, and his eyes bore into me. I concentrate on a spot, a single hair, low on his chest for an aiming point. It's an easy heart shot at this distance. He'll die quickly.

He swings his head side to side, then snaps his sharp canine teeth together in a rapid series of loud, hollow clacks. It's the same warning sound I've heard from an enraged wild boar.

The hollowness of the sound penetrates my soul, and my fingers cannot loose the shaft. My eyes leave the spot over his heart, and I look into his small black eyes.

He lifts his front paw, then sets it down, gingerly. He doesn't run. His head swings from side to side and he snaps another warning. The sound touches me again. My feeling isn't fear, but the hollowness of the time of burning. He's been through too much. I've been through too much. Flooded with weary empathy for the animal, I lower my bow.

We stand a few feet apart, staring at each other, each of us vulnerable. His refusal to run, the sound of his teeth snapping together, remind me of the death of our valley. His actions destroy my desire to kill.

We remain motionless, appraising each other, knowing one could kill the other. Then he shuffles across the road through the trees and climbs a ten-foot-high boulder next to the granite cliff. I follow, not to stalk him for another opportunity for a shot nor for any logical reason. When I'm twenty yards from the boulder, I sit down and lean against an aspen tree. My longbow rests in my lap. The bear stands on the flat top of the boulder and watches me, then lies down.

We watch each other for a long time. Finally, he puts his head on his front paws, and minutes later, closes his eyes. He's exhausted. I watch him and wonder how far he fled in front of the flames. How did he survive? When had he last eaten?

I fight to keep my eyes from closing, but nod off.

Sometime later, I'm startled awake by a touch on my shoulder. Standing over me is the leader of a Native American hotshot fire crew. Two black braids hang beside his face. He wears a fire-fighter's yellow shirt. I see his necklace of bear claws and think I'm dreaming. The rest of his crew stands silent on the driveway. The man holds his finger to his lips in the universal gesture for silence.

He points to the bear on the rock, then my bow. He raises his right arm and makes the motion of shooting.

I shake my head, no.

His fingers touch his bear claw necklace and he nods. He straightens, turns, and motions his crew to follow him up the drive-way.

I look at the sleeping bear, then at the hotshot fire crew walking single file toward Lake Creek, where another spot fire must have broken out.

I rise and follow them.

I see the bear one more time. His picture is on the front page of the Cody weekly newspaper. The picture was taken near Lake Creek, later on the same day that I saw him. Tongue hanging out, he is sprawled upside down in the back of a pickup truck. The grinning hunter, with his scoped rifle, poses over him.

It breaks my heart.

# YOU WOULDN'T

"Get away! Get away!" Tish, my five-foot-two-inch wife, bounds down the stepping stones toward the two mule deer bucks who are nibbling her spring flowers. The bucks, emerging antlers in velvet, look at her. A yellow daisy hangs from the lips of the wide-antlered one. She waves her arms over her head and charges them. The bread-basket-antlered buck stomps his front hoof. Tish stops. It's a Mexican standoff.

I watch the bucks throughout the spring. The wide-antlered buck grows into a four point. His bread-basket buddy's antlers have grown into five points on the right and four on the left. I know by fall they will be trophies. I've never killed a trophy mule deer. They let me approach within twenty yards before trotting off. I stalk them every day. They ignore me. Perfect.

"I love to watch wild animals, but those two bucks are just too much. They're ruining my garden, I wish we could do something," Tish says one evening.

"Yeah, I know what you mean, honey." I smile. I'm getting older and it might not be strictly sportsmanlike to eat a pet, but what the heck.

One morning, during the first week of August, I stand near the bucks while they feed on Tish's flowers. I raise my pretend bow, draw an imaginary arrow, aim, and release. My only problem is deciding which buck will look better hanging on my wall. I figure they'll taste the same, sort of like daisies and violets.

At that moment, Tish walks up behind me. "What are you doing?" The wide-antlered buck looks at us.

I can't lie. "Uh . . . pretending it's hunting season."

Bread-basket buck's head snaps up.

"You wouldn't shoot one of those bucks?" She can't believe I'd stoop to killing a pet.

The bucks' feet shuffle, tails twitch.

"Not until hunting season," I say with resolve, yet I feel a touch of shame.

The bucks bound off, jump the buck-and-rail fence, and in spite of spending all of bow season hunting for them, I never see them again.

# DANCING IN THE MOONLIGHT

Wet. Shivering. I stagger through knee-deep snow, following the tracks of my sheep hunting guide, Bob Woodward. A full moon rises, bathing me in its frigid brilliance. Snow-ladened pines tower over the trail. A hand grasps my elbow—maybe it's my imagination.

"John?" Bob's voice is cold and distant.

I shuffle on, bending under the weight of my pack and rifle.

"John? Are you okay?" Bob's voice drifts from the shadows to my left. Maybe it's the shadow talking. I'm too tired to look.

"Yeah," I mumble. My voice echoes the violent shivering of my body.

"There's a trapper's cabin up ahead. You've got to make it to that cabin. It's too cold to camp out tonight." His voice is sharp.

"Cold . . ." My teeth chatter.

"I'll walk ahead to break trail."

171

"Walk . . ." I feel his hand on my shoulder, a cold squeeze, then watch him pull away like a powerful locomotive leaving me at the station.

His tracks form a straight black shadow that cuts the downy white. I lurch from one side of his tracks to the other.

My hands shake when I try to feel my face. A welcome cold fog smothers my brain, suffocates my senses.

In a magical transformation, the snow-burdened pines turn into palm trees. I halt to watch the miracle. The frigid full moon becomes the fiery sun. Waves of heat wash my body. I'm in awe of the spectacle and stop shivering. I smile, drop my rifle, then my backpack.

The warmth is wonderful! I strip off my coat and lie on my back in the hot sun on the warm sand beach. Wonderful! I drift into a peaceful sleep.

"John! . . . . John!"

"Leave me alone," I mutter and wave the voice away.

Hands grab the front of my shirt and shake. The sun and sand and heat disappear, replaced by moon and snow and cold.

"You can't quit now, the cabin is close," Bob screams.

I grin and nod my head and flop back in the snow in an effort to regain the warmth.

"Get up!" He pulls me to my feet. I weave like a punch-drunk fighter.

He puts my coat back on.

"Don't wanta go," my distant voice mutters.

"I'll carry your pack and rifle, but you've got to follow right behind me. Do it!" Bob's voice sounds urgent, but I don't give a damn.

He lashes my backpack over his, then shoulders my rifle. He looks funny, grotesque. He grabs my arm and pushes me forward.

I will the moon to turn back into the sun, but it remains a cold orb in the starlit void. I begin shivering again and stagger onward.

Bob leads me to the window of the trapper's cabin, leans me against the log wall, then strips off the backpacks and rifle. I collapse, slide down the wall, and sink into snow up to my chest. Warm. Sleepy.

He forces his belt knife between the window jam and frame and feels for the latch to unlock it.

"Got it!" Bob opens the window, climbs into the dark cabin, then returns to drag me over the windowsill. I flop on the floor of the one-room shack.

He gets my down sleeping bag out, strips me naked, and lays me next to a barrel-shaped wood stove in the middle of the room. The fire in the stove becomes so hot that I can see through the cherry-red metal, but I shiver until I drift off.

My first sight the next morning is Bob stoking the fire. He smiles.

"You going to make it?" he asks.

I feel like someone cut out all my muscles while I slept. "Thanks for last night," I mutter.

He spends the day feeding wood to the fire, feeding me soup and water to hydrate my body. I spend the day curled in a fetal position inside my down sleeping bag, embarrassed.

"You had a bad case of hypothermia," he said.

"I guess."

"How'd it feel?" he asks.

"Wet, exhausted, freezing, shivering, but after a certain point it was pleasant. I wanted to drift off."

"Yeah, and never come back," Bob says in a serious tone of voice.

"Cold out?" I ask.

"Twenty or thirty below."

"Cold." I shiver, roll into a tight ball, and sleep.

It's dusk when I wake. I watch Bob use an old-fashioned can opener to punch a can open with a series of triangular cuts. He gingerly raises the jagged star-shaped top, so he doesn't cut his fingers. Then he dumps the contents into a pot on the wood stove, folds the sharp top back into the can, and sets it on the floor next to the stove. I'm immersed in the smell of something cooking. I doze, then feel his hand on my shoulder.

"Chicken stew. You need to drink more water," Bob says, handing me another cup.

I raise to my elbow and drink, then he hands me a bowl of stew. I don't want to talk. I talked this sheep hunting game warden into guiding me, his first hunter, then I get soaked by rain which turned to snow, get exhausted and hypothermic. I put both our lives in danger. He'll probably never take anyone else hunting.

A beam of cold moonlight angles through the window to flood the cabin. I hear Bob's soft snoring. It must be the middle of the night, and I've got to pee, bad. I snake out of my sleeping bag, swing my feet to the floor, and hope Bob doesn't see me naked. I don't know where he put my clothes. I jerk my feet off the ice-cold floor and weigh my options. The snow is deep. It's far below freezing. I have to cross the floor, open the door, wade naked into knee-deep snow to take a whiz.

I see a better solution. The empty chicken stew can lies on the floor next to the stove. I can use it to pee in, then toss it out in the morning, after I find my clothes.

I tiptoe to the stove, pick up the can, hoping that Bob's not watching this naked specter in the moonlight, and begin peeing in the can. My stream makes a tinkling noise that'll wake him up, so I stick my penis deep into the can, past its sharp star-shaped top, and tip the can to soften the noise. I look over my shoulder. His eyes are closed. I don't want to embarrass him.

What a relief! I'm finished and begin to pull out of the can when I'm caught by the arrow-shaped top. Ouch! I can't get it out. I stand next to the stove, squirming one way then another, like a naked male belly dancer, trying to extract myself from the can.

Finally! Finally, I'm free. I set the can on the floor next to my bunk and slide back into my sleeping bag and lie awake all night trying to think up good excuses if, in the morning, Bob asks, "What in the hell were you doing, dancing naked in the moonlight?"

He doesn't.

# THE SHIRTTAIL BUCK

Hunting buddy Bob Pletz and I are speeding down a lonely stretch of State Highway 70, thirteen miles west of Florence, Wisconsin, when our conversation dies a comfortable death. I flip on the radio, tune to a Duluth station, and hear frantic news: President Kennedy has been assassinated.

We can hear grief in the announcer's voice, "Trucks are pulled off to the side of the highway here. Burly truckers are sobbing like babies . . ."

"Not the day before deer season in northern Wisconsin," Bob observes. He's driving my old Plymouth station wagon, crammed with our rifles, wool coats, winter boots, duffels, and other gear.

A pickup passes us. Three men wearing red hunting hats sit in its front seat. A fat guy sitting next to the passenger door grins and tips his can of Bud in a salute. Our speedometer reads eighty.

Bob chuckles. "No, sir! No one's pulling over up here."

I look at Bob and wonder how he can be irreverent upon hearing a national tragedy, but irreverent humor is his essence. The guy can find humor in any situation.

I remember the old saying about humor being the child of pain. Bob must have experienced a lot of pain because he's the funniest guy I know. I've known him since high school, and I can't figure out what spawned his sense of humor.

Sometimes his offbeat wit makes me feel a tad uncomfortable, but it doesn't seem to affect other people that way. Bob worms his way into everyone's heart. I've watched him work a four A.M. miracle with a cynical waitress tired of groping drunks and hungover hunters. Somehow, Bob connected on a gut level and left her with a grin on her face.

The frantic news on the radio fades while I think about Bob. I have mixed feelings about asking him to join me at Chuck Thompson's annual deer hunt. Chuck and I played football in college and my first invitation to hunt deer at his father's old farm had been during my sophomore year. As the years rolled by the older generation of hunters died off, and now the camp is populated each deer season by Chuck and some of his close buddies. It's a close-knit group, and I'm not sure how they'll accept Bob.

The reason that I'm nervous is that while Bob's sense of humor makes him friends easily, he's a big-city boy. He's soft and walks clumsily, and his eyelids have big white patches that sometimes makes him look like an owl. He can be a klutz in the woods. Yet he's big-hearted and always carries a shit-eating grin and is lightning-fast with wisecracks. I love him, but I hope he won't embarrass me with the gang.

At dusk, I direct Bob down a snow-packed dirt road that snakes between evergreen forests and abandoned farm fields until we pull up to Charlie's dilapidated farmhouse. Snow scrunches under our tires as we park between an old Ford pickup and a couple of sedans.

Bob turns off the engine. The snow, herded across a twenty-acre plowed field by a howling wind, lashes the unpainted wood siding of the house. "Man, let's get inside. I really gotta go!"

"We don't have plumbing, Bob." I struggle into my coat before opening the door.

"No plumbing?" Bob looks incredulous.

"An outhouse. I'll show you." I pull down the ear flaps on my red hunting cap and slip on my gloves, then open the door and step into the storm. Bob follows me through ankle-deep snow as I curl around the corner of the porch toward the outhouse. There are no tracks in the snow.

The outhouse leans against the wind at the edge of the field. The snow beats against it with savage ferocity.

"Jeeze," Bob mutters.

I turn the wooden latch and open the door for him. The outhouse's two holes are rough-cut into the single wooden plank that serves as the seat. Snow jettisons out of the twin holes like icy exhaust from jet engines. Two columns of snow hit the slanted ceiling, then billow down the walls to pile along the edges.

Bob's eyes widen. "I'll wait."

I introduce Bob to three-hundred-pound Charlie and the rest of the gang in the kitchen, which is filled with the smell of frying meat and coffee and other good things. My stomach rumbles.

"We're sitting down to a dinner of steaks and fried potatoes, John. Eat first, then you guys can drag your gear inside."

A gas lantern hangs from a wire over the center of the round table that is covered with a blue plastic tablecloth.

Bob notices colorful pieces of cloth nailed high on the walls, next to the fly-specked ceiling. "What're those, Charlie?"

Charlie stops chewing on a chunk of steak and mumbles, "Shirttails."

"Oh." Bob looks at me and raises his left eyebrow.

Charlie sees the motion and swallows. "We've got this tradition here. Any hunter who misses a buck gets his shirttail cut off and nailed up there." He points with his fork.

"Of course." Bob struggles for something funny to say, but I think he's intimidated.

Charlie pours coffee out of a huge enamel-plated pot that has been steaming on the wood stove.

"John, we've got a full house, so you and Bob have to sleep in the double bed upstairs. Hope you boys don't mind sleeping together." A grin spreads across Charlie's face.

Bob jumps right in. "Naw, Charlie. On the way up, John and I talked about getting engaged. Probably get it done tonight."

I feel heat rise in my face, and I hope my hollow laugh is lost in the guffawing and bellowing. Bob's comment starts an avalanche of jokes. He's passed the first test.

Later, after we'd hauled our stuff to the second-floor bedroom, selected the side of the bed we wanted to sleep on, and suffered the ribald taunts of our companions, we turn out our lantern and slip under the heavy blankets and quilts. The old mattress sags and within seconds our butts kiss. Silent and embarrassed, I claw my way to the edge of the mattress, hook my right knee over its edge and hold on.

The next time Bob moves the bed collapses onto the floor, and we're thrown into each other's arms. The darkened house erupts with shrieks of laughter, whooping, and hollering. We laugh and try to ignore the taunts and good-natured insults. Since I've been to hunting camp many times, I figure this is Bob's initiation. I'm happy the guys accept him.

Sleep is shattered in the middle of the night by Charlie's booming voice, "Daylight in the swamp! Rise and shine! Daylight in the swamp!"

We cook a breakfast of fried ham and bacon, eggs, toast, and coffee, then bundle up and, rifles in hand, walk outside. I stand on the porch and look at the sky. No stars, but the wind has died.

Charlie plays the beam of his flashlight across fresh snow and it looks like the reflection of millions of diamonds. "Better get going, don't want to miss dawn. John, you put Bob on John-O's stand. Don't let him get lost."

The snow is now calf-deep and so dry that I can't hear my own footsteps, much less Bob's, who trudges close behind. We skirt the west edge of the field, then hook left at the old two-forked pine and slough through the evergreens in light snow for twenty minutes. My flashlight picks up tracks.

"Look, Bob, deer tracks. Came through this morning. Maybe a buck." My heart is thumping with excitement. If I could only help get Bob his first buck.

Bob ignores the deer track. "Where are you going to be?"

"Huh?"

"After you put me on John-O's stand . . . where are you going?"

That's the problem with city boys. They feel comfortable when surrounded by killer gangs but aren't confident enough to follow their own tracks back to the farmhouse.

"I'll be close, but out of rifle shot, along the edge of the swamp you'll be facing. The deer like to skirt the edge."

Ten minutes later, we arrive at the huge pine whose top had snapped off and fallen, a perfect ambush spot. I point with my flashlight.

"This is John-O's stand. Brush the snow off that limb and use it for a seat. The swamp's about seventy yards in front of you. Make sure you see horns before you pull the trigger."

"Yeah . . ." Bob doesn't move.

"You got a light?" I ask.

He nods.

"Okay. I'm going to take a stand a couple hundred yards down that way. Stay here. I'll come back to pick you up about ten."

"Yeah . . . " He still doesn't move.

I turn and slip silent feet through the snow. It's glorious. The snow sparkles from the beam of my light. Evergreen branches droop under their fresh white blankets. Black shadows of tree trunks spin around me like ghostly specters at a macabre dance.

Maybe it's the fleeting shadows that make me shiver. A black thought scuds across my mind. I'm not alone; something else, something evil, is descending upon me. I stop and cast my light from side to side. Its beam knifes the ink-black night. I think I see a movement near a tree to the left, but when my light floods out the shadows there is nothing. So why do I grip my rifle tighter?

I feel the weight of my rifle and think the 180-grain .30–06 Silvertip bullet won't stop the things my imagination conjures. I shake my head to rid myself of this stupid image and trek on, slicing through death-quiet snow.

A few minutes later, I'm seized by the feeling that something is gaining on me. I halt. Certain the terror is creeping up behind me, I spin and shine my light and spot eyes, white teeth, and round face. Three feet behind me stands Bob, with a shit-eating grin on his face.

"Wh . . . what the hell are you doing?" I pant.

"I thought you might get lost," he says.

"You scared the hell out of me! Could'a shot you." I look at my watch. There isn't time to take him back to his tree, so I take him to my stand. We stand together, silent, under the branches of an immense pine and welcome the leaden gray of dawn. I'm seething, yet there's a certain comfort that he's there. At least I know he can't get into trouble.

We hear far-off shots, but nothing moves near us. At ten, I suggest that we head back to the warmth of the wood stove.

"We'll go a different way, Bob. Be quiet. Maybe we'll kick up a bedded buck."

There's a little valley to our right, and we quietly walk up its slope toward the field. A movement to our left. I halt. I make out the tips of a buck's rack, then the form of his bedded body comes into view. It's a perfect shot for Bob.

I touch Bob's arm and whisper, "Fifty yards to the left, Bob. He's bedded under the branches of that huge pine. Shoot him."

"Where?" Bob asks in a voice that shatters the silence of the woods.

"There. Under the tree . . . No, no, to the left. To the left!" My voice rises.

Bob cranes his head and sees everything but the buck.

"Shoot!" I hiss.

"Where?" Bob hasn't even brought his rifle up.

The buck, watching us, then dips his head as if to get up. Bob doesn't see it. Fearing a lost opportunity, I raise my rifle, put the crosshairs of my scope on the buck's neck and squeeze the trigger. My shot echoes through the woods.

"Oh, there!" Bob says, looking at the fallen buck.

He holds its back legs while I begin field-dressing the deer. As I roll its intestines onto the snow, a branch behind us breaks. I look back to see two more bucks jogging directly toward us, following the track of the buck I killed.

"Get your rifle, Bob! Here come two bucks." I point.

Bob jumps for his rifle and watches the bucks approach.

"Shoot! Shoot," I whisper.

Bob watches the bucks trot past, then raises his rifle and snaps off a wild shot as they disappear behind the trees.

"Looks like you're going to lose your shirttail." I laugh. Might as well make fun out of this fiasco, I think.

At the dinner table that night, Charlie, primed for the task, calls for a trial. I'm the star witness. I don't tell the first part of the story, the part about Bob following me, but I tell the truth about Bob's blunder with the two bucks.

Charlie pushes back his chair, ambles to the kitchen counter, opens the drawer, and pulls out a large pair of shears. He sets them, with a great act of ceremony, in front of his plate and says, "It's time for a vote for Bob's shirttail."

"Wait! Wait!" cries Bob. "Doesn't the accused get to say something for his own defense?"

Charlie leans back in his creaking chair and grins. "Okay, Bob. What'd ya got to say for yourself?"

"Well," Bob says with a somber face, "you all know this is my first time deer hunting and . . . well . . . I was waiting to shoot until my buck bedded down like John's."

Charlie leads the uproarious laughter, then pronounces, "Case against Bob Pletz . . . dismissed."

# NEWFOUNDLAND
# IMAGES

"I am not going to shoot the first bull caribou I see. I'm going to take my time, look them over," Jerry Mason says when we get into the guide's boat for a short trip across the lake to hunt the tundra. He cradles his .54-caliber muzzleloader close to his body so it won't get wet.

"You're repeating yourself." I laugh.

"I know, but caribou antlers look huge. It's easy to get excited and shoot a small bull. I'm going to take my time to hunt for a trophy."

"I'll be happy if I can stalk close to a decent animal for a shot with my longbow."

"I have an idea, John. Since your shooting range is under thirty yards and I can be effective out to a hundred and twenty, why don't we hunt together? If we see a bull we both want, you put a stalk on him first and I'll back you up. If you can't complete your stalk, I'll have a chance."

"Doesn't seem fair to you, Jerry, but if that's what you want to do, let's try it."

Two hours later, we spot the first mature bull caribou feeding alone across the rock-strewn tundra pocked with ponds and lakes. We huddle behind a large boulder about a hundred and fifty yards from the bull. Jerry sets up his spotting scope and studies the animal. I look at him through my binoculars.

"It looks like a good bull to me, Jerry. I'd like to try for him. What do you think?"

"I'm not sure. His right horn has eight points and the left has ten, but his left bez looks weak." Jerry focuses the scope to further study the bull.

"Pretty good bull," our guide, Tom, says.

"Yeah, but he's the first mature bull we've seen. Why don't you try for him, John?" Jerry asks.

"It's too barren for a stalk. I'll spook him."

Tom looks at me. "The wind's blowing in the right direction. Caribou are curious. Bend over and hold your longbow over your head like horns. I'll put my hands on your back and walk behind you. We'll walk directly toward him, and maybe he'll think we're a strange-looking caribou."

"Sounds good. Sure you don't want to try for him, Jerry?" I ask.

"No. I'll stay here and watch." Jerry still studies the bull's antlers through his spotting scope.

The guide and I creep across the tundra, stop, go, stop, and go. Each time we stop I lower my head and bow, pretending to feed on the short grasses.

We are fifty yards from the bull when his head snaps up to look at us. He stares, then lifts his nose high to scent this strange apparition feeding close to him. His nostrils flare. We're downwind so he can't scent us. Too far for a shot.

He walks in a slow arc to our right in an effort to get the wind in his favor and widens the distance between us. Now he's eighty yards away and about a hundred yards from the rock where Jerry is watching.

It will be a matter of seconds before the bull smells us and spooks.

*Ka-boom!* The bull staggers. A cloud of smoke drifts upward from the rock. Over the top of the boulder, I see Jerry's right arm pumping up and down. He's reloading his muzzleloader. He shoots again and the bull drops dead, a bullet through his heart.

Jerry measures the distance from the rock, a hundred and ten yards.

"I didn't think you were going to shoot the first bull, Jerry." I grin and shake his hand.

Jerry measures the bull's antlers and discovers the bull will go number one for woodland caribou in the muzzleloader record book.

I take Jerry's picture and think about a guy who'd give his hunting buddy first chance at a record-book animal. He's a true sportsman.

We hunt for five more days, but I can't get close enough to a bull for a shot. On the last morning, we spot a nice bull and I make a stalk. I'm on my knees, with my chest on the ground, pretending to be a rock when he walks past at thirty yards.

"This is my last chance," I think as I rise and draw the arrow. The bull jumps the string and the arrow misses the lungs.

The bull runs a couple hundred yards and lies down, sick.

"Shoot him again! Shoot him again!" the guide urges.

"No. We'll let him lay. In a couple hours, he'll die in peace," I say.

"No. No! Finish him off now!"

He should know the behavior of woodland caribou. I listen to him. It's my second mistake.

The bull rises when I creep within sixty-five yards and looks like he's going to bolt. I arc an arrow toward him and miss. Filled with adrenaline, the white-maned bull staggers across the tundra.

Vowing not to leave an animal wounded by my hand, I follow for hours, miss three more shots. The arrows bury deep in the tundra and disappear. I have one left. I feel like vomiting.

The bull stands on the edge of a lake. Water is a caribou's favorite method of escape. He watches me.

I ask Jerry and Tom, who have witnessed this terrible ordeal, to return to camp for more arrows. I just can't allow this magnificent animal to suffer a lingering death.

The bull walks into the water and starts swimming to the far shore. I sprint around the edge of the lake and just as I realize I can't get to the other shore ahead of him, he turns and swims directly toward me.

I hide behind a bush and wait. And wait. When he's twenty yards from shore, I shoot my last arrow. And miss.

I throw my bow down, bolt into the water, grab the bull's thrashing antlers against my chest and push his head underwater. I hold onto the wildly thrashing animal until I feel his life's energy ebb.

I drag his lifeless body from the water, fall to my knees next to his head, and cry, "I'm sorry! I'm sorry."

# WOOD RIVER

"Be careful!" I shout to my young sheep hunting guide. He adjusts his metal-frame pack, then takes a running start to jump over the crevasse on Alaska's Wood River Glacier. We're camped below the glacier and use it as a highway to locate Dall rams in the surrounding mountains. Several times each day he jumps these wide cracks that plunge hundreds of feet out of sight into eerie blue ice.

Falling into a crevasse is a terrible way to die. Crevasses are shaped like a V, wide at the top and narrow at the bottom. When a man falls, his body wedges between walls of ice. Gradually, his body heat melts a bit of ice and he slips down inch by inch, then suffocates to death, slowly. But eighteen-year-olds don't think about dying.

His jumping makes me feel like a chicken, but I've got three little kids and a lovely wife at home. I detour a long way around each crevasse. I start my detour.

"AH-E-E-E-E-e-e-e-e-e-e!"

I look back to see him, arms flailing, fall backward and disappear into the crevasse. I feel sick. I run back to where he fell, get on my hands and knees, crawl to the edge, and look down. He lies on his back, feet and arms up, suspended in a narrow chute, several feet down. His metal backpack is wedged into the walls of the crevasse.

"Help," he begs softly, as if using a loud voice will jar him loose and plummet him to his death.

"I've got you." I lie on my stomach, reach down for his hand, and pray he doesn't pull me down with him.

His hand rises toward mine. Our fingers are inches apart. I can't lean over farther without losing my balance. I wish I had a rope or a pole . . . that's it!

"We'll use my longbow." I scramble to where I'd dropped my bow, take it to the edge, and start lowering it to him, then stop.

"Give me the bow!" he pleads as his fingers grasp for it.

"No. If I pull you up this way, all your weight will be on the bow. If I can get to the other side, you can use your feet to leverage out."

"Oh, God!" he whispers.

I drop my day pack and run up the glacier until I find a narrow place to jump across, then, using my pack as a marker, run back.

"Grab my bow and plant your feet against the wall of the crevasse."

He does and I pull. Nothing happens. The frame of his backpack is jammed in the ice.

"You've got to jerk your body to free it. Hold the bow tight!" It's cold on the ice, but sweat pours down my face.

He jerks his shoulder, the metal frame loosens and, holding the bow, he climbs out of the crevasse. We fall on the ice, panting.

"Please don't tell Dad about this," he pleads. His dad, back in Fairbanks, is the outfitter.

"On one condition," I say.

"What?"

"That you stop jumping those damned crevasses!"

He grins and sticks out his hand to seal our agreement.

Each day we get within seventy or eighty yards of big rams, but the country is open, and I can't get close enough for a killing shot. I'm not about to take a shot unless I'm certain of a quick kill.

Two days after the crevasse accident, we stalk within a hundred yards of a band of seven good rams. The leader climbs a steep slope, digs out a bed, and lies down. He watches while the others follow his example, one by one, according to horn size, the largest to the smallest.

A half hour later, the leader looks at the next largest, gets up, saunters behind his buddy, strikes him in the butt with a front hoof until the ram gets up, then the big ram takes his bed.

The second largest ram, evicted from his spot, turns to the next largest after him and does the same thing. Within twenty minutes the smallest ram is looking for a new spot. He eyes the vacated bed of the leader, then digs himself a new bed and lies down.

"Now I understand the meaning of 'pecking order,'" I whisper.

On the last morning, we break camp and backpack down the river to base camp, which is an eight-by-twelve-foot shack containing a couple of bunks and a woodstove. Not fancy, but it'll keep you out of the rain.

The next morning, my guide and I watch his dad's Super Cub buzz the gravel bar on the river next to the camp.

"Remember your promise not to tell Dad about my fall." The young man looks me in the eyes.

"You kept your promise, I'll keep mine," I say, watching the Super Cub turn for a final approach and bounce on its fat tundra tires to a stop next to us. I'm surprised to see a woman in the back seat.

The outfitter opens the door, helps her out. "This is my wife. We're going to spend a couple days up here after I take you boys back."

She's so good-looking that I yearn for my wife, Tish.

"My son has a doctor's appointment, so I'll fly him out first. I'll be back in two and a half hours to pick you up."

Wife and I watch them take off and disappear down valley, then she takes her gear into the shack. I decide to grab my bow and take a walk.

Two hours later, returning to the shack, I watch fog roll up the valley. It looks like a gigantic steamroller bearing down upon us. The outfitter won't be able to fly through that.

"How long will it last?" I ask his wife.

"It's a little early for this, but I've seen it sock in for as long as a week," she says.

"Oh!"

Three days later, an evening breeze lifts the fog, and the next morning we hear the Super Cub's engine, then watch it land.

The outfitter gets out and hurries to the shack.

"Sorry I couldn't get back for you. It was fogged in all the way to Fairbanks."

"That's okay," I say.

"You guys been okay?" he asks, looking at his wife.

"Fine." She smiles.

The outfitter turns to me. "Oh, by the way, John. Your wife, Tish, called last night."

"What'd she say?"

"She said you were supposed to be home day before yesterday. She hasn't heard from you and was worried. I said, 'You
think you're worried? John's been up in camp alone for three
days with my wife!' "

# YUKON IMAGES

Snowbound three days, curled under a green plastic tarp. Shivering.

I brush a foot of snow off my sleeping bag to peer through the night at the silhouette of the silent Indian huddled next to the fire. Day after day, night after night. It's his first hunt as a guide. He used the topographic map as fire starter. I'm doomed.

I hope my hunting partner, Jerry Mason, is warm. His guide was smart to pack a canvas wall tent on their hunt for mountain caribou. His guide asked mine if he wanted to pack the other wall tent for our trip.

"Don't need it for two-day moose hunt," my guide said.

I could have insisted but figured these guides live in this country. They know what they need. We were going to hunt separate areas, camping where night found us. We'd soon return to hunt together out of our main camp.

Jerry's warm. I know it. Hope so. Wish I were with him.

Five days ago, Jerry missed a white arctic wolf, because he got so excited he forgot to put an ignition cap on his muzzle-loader. Then his horse shied and he ripped his hamstring, which turned black and blue.

I felt sorry for the man I met almost thirty years ago while waiting for his pilot to load the floatplane on the shore of Mow-dade Lake, British Columbia. Jerry has become a friend.

The next day my guide moves from the fire, finds the horses, and we pack up. The horses break a chest-deep trail through snow to camp, where Jerry and his guide wait.

The following day the bullet of Jerry's muzzleloader falls short of a giant moose because the bullet loosened and slipped partway down the barrel while in the rifle scabbard on the horse.

When the snow stops the lake next to camp freezes solid. Our outfitter can't pick us up in the floatplane.

It's a two-day-long, frigid horseback ride back to base camp. Frozen reins, frozen saddles, frozen fingers.

"I can't wait to come back," says Jerry.

# ALASKA IMAGES

"Why does the map call that Three Day Mountain?" my son John asks from the bow of our canoe. The river slows, coils and winds, and coils and winds. It takes us three days to paddle past the darned mountain.

Later, photographing big game animals in Denali National Park, I wake one early morning to discover John, a college senior, isn't in his sleeping bag. Last night he bumped into an acquaintance from college. I don't blame him.

On a layover in Fairbanks, we rent a hotel room, shower, and go to the laundromat.

"Dad, you can't wash those wool pants."

"Sure can," I insist. I toss them into the washing machine and slam the lid. Damn kid thinks he knows everything.

"They'll shrink," he says, cocksure.

I jam quarters into the machine and give John a dirty look when I punch the start button.

When I pull them out of the washer, he looks over the top of his magazine and says, "I'm telling ya, Dad, if you put them in the dryer, they're gonna shrink for sure."

I ram quarters into the dryer and punch the start button. An hour later, I put on the pants. The bottom of the legs reach my calf.

"Just the way I like them," I say.

A day later, after I've cooled down, we're horsepacking into a cabin on the Wood River for a self-guided bowhunt for caribou.

"They migrate across the flat and cross that ridge but never follow the same path. Be sure to keep that shotgun with you. There are lots of bears out here. Good luck," our outfitter says when he leaves us.

That night I'm startled by John's screams.

"What is it?" I grab our shotgun.

"Don't know. Something big and furry brushed across my face." John stands on his bunk and shines his flashlight around the cabin.

I'm ready with the shotgun. We finally shine the light under his bunk to find a frightened weasel. We laugh, open the door, and he scampers into the dark.

There are no caribou the next day, but we notice our boots are stained blue.

"Blueberries!" I say, looking down at a huge patch of ripe blueberries. We fall to our knees, fill my hat with the fruit, and make a blueberry pie for dinner.

Several days later, caribou trickle through on the start of their annual migration. We hide on the far side of the ridge, watch them cross the flat, and when we see a good bull, try to ambush him by guessing where he'll top over the ridge. Invariably, they change their minds when we're not looking and crest the ridge thirty or forty yards too far for a clean shot.

"Maybe we'll have a better chance if we split up. Why don't you take your bow and the shotgun and climb up the ridge about three hundred yards," I suggest.

An hour later, I see John spring up and start jumping up and down. What the heck is he doing? He knows better than to skyline himself.

He raises his arms above his head and frantically jumps up and down. I look at him through my binoculars; he's shouting something, but the wind is fierce, and I can't hear him.

Arms high over his head, he bends his knees and does a macabre dance. Maybe he's constipated. In any event, the kid's going to spook every caribou in Alaska.

He bends over, grabs the shotgun, and sprints down the ridge toward me.

"Hey! Hey! Hey!" His shouts reach me.

"Hey, yourself." I stand up and wave at him. We've been too long in the bush.

He runs to me, breathless. He looks around. "Didn't you see them?"

"See what?"

"There were three huge grizzlies stalking you. I was trying to warn you. They got as close as that bush over there before they heard me and ran off." John pointed to a bush forty yards away.

I had been stalking caribou while grizzlies were stalking me. The predator was the prey.

My stomach starts to churn. I take a deep breath and exhale slowly. Then I put my arm around my son's shoulders and squeeze hard.

"Thanks," I say, scanning the mountainside for the three bears. I can't see them, but know they are out there, waiting.

# WHAT DID SHE SAY?

"I couldn't hear a word she said. I mirrored her body language; when she smiled, I smiled. When she looked serious, I looked serious. I don't know whether she said she had breast cancer, or her kid won the Nobel," I told my wife, Tish, on the drive home from the dinner party.

"Maybe you should investigate hearing aids," she said.

Now, six months later, standing at the sink in my room at the hunting lodge on an Alberta black bear hunt, I look at the disgusting brown hearing aids that I've avoided wearing and decide it might be time to try them out; they could help me hear the stealthy footsteps of a bruin approaching my tree stand.

I stick the darned things in my ears and, hoping Nic Patrick, my hunting partner, and the other hunters don't notice the translucent handles that stick out of my ears, walk out to join them under the shade of maple trees next to the lake.

"Hi." My voice sounds like it echoes from some deep cave. I wonder whether that's what my real voice sounds like, or if it's an amplified version.

"Grab a Pepsi and join us," Nic says, pointing to an empty chair.

I walk to the cooler, pick out a can, and pop it open. Its loud *swoosh* startles me, but it doesn't foam over the top. I join the guys, who are telling about their morning hunts.

I hear the raucous singing of a flock of birds in the trees above us. "Wow! Listen to that. The birds must have started their migration south," I say.

The guys exchange puzzled looks.

"Huh?" Nic asks.

"Don't you hear all those birds? Must have just flown in. They weren't here earlier," I say.

"Sure they were, John. They've been here since we arrived yesterday," Nic says.

"Oh. Guess I wasn't paying attention," I mumble. The darned hearing aids must work, I think. I can hardly wait to get up into the tree stand for the evening hunt. Hearing will add an entirely new dimension to my bear hunting.

Several hours later I am amazed at the amount of sound I make as I climb into the tree stand. Every time I shift position my clothes sound like the roar of a waterfall. All the noise will scare every animal out of the woods, I think, but soon squirrels appear and chase each other up and down my tree. Their scampering sounds like a squad of army tanks. A sparrow lands on a branch next to my shoulder and chirps loudly.

The hearing aids jam too much sound into my head. I can't stand it. I slip them into my pocket and wait for a bear.

An hour later, a bear sneaks in, silent. My arrow flies straight, and he bounds off, disappearing into the thick brush. I listen for the thrashing of brush, but all I hear is silence. Is he lying dead, or still running, or waiting to attack his pursuer? I wish I'd left the darned hearing aids in my ears.

Toby, our outfitter, a big, tough-looking guy, told us when we arrived in camp, "If you shoot a bear, stay in the tree. I don't want you down on the ground chasing a bear through the thick brush. Wait until I pick you up. I'll have a shotgun and will help you track the bear. I don't want a mauled hunter in my camp."

I wait until Toby returns, then climb out of the tree and tell him I've shot a bear. He pulls out his shotgun, chambers a round of buckshot. I shove my hearing aids back into my ears and take Toby to the spot where I'd hit the bear. We find a blood trail.

"Was it a killing shot?" he asks.

Sure, I think, but it's a bear and they're big and dangerous. I don't want him to be careless, so I say, "I think so, but the bear spun away so fast I didn't get a good look at the arrow placement. Could have been a little high."

"Did you hear him fall in the brush . . . a death rattle?" he asks.

"No, I didn't hear anything," I say.

We find the blood trail, heavy at first. Twenty yards into the thick brush the blood trail turns to occasional drops. My hearing aids magnify our footsteps, snapping twigs sound like falling trees. The drumbeat of my heart sounds like I'm standing between two bass drums. My ears are plugged with the darned hearing aids, which makes me dizzy. I pull them out again and jam them into my pants pocket. I'll rely on my eyes.

"You watch in front for the bear. I'll follow the blood." Toby drops to his hands and knees to look for blood on the grass. He shoves the shotgun ahead of him. I walk next to him, searching for signs ahead.

When he crawls close to a fallen tree trunk that blocks our path, I spot a patch of black fur, the hip of the bear. Its shoulders and head are hidden by the tree.

"There he is!" I whisper. I string an arrow and aim at the fur patch, waiting for it to move. I know the arrow won't stop a charging bear, but it might distract it long enough to give Toby a fatal shot.

Toby rises to his knees, grabs his shotgun in both hands, and swings its muzzle in an arc in front of him. "Where? Where?"

"Just in front of you. On the other side of that tree trunk," I say.

The outfitter shoulders his shotgun and aims at the top edge of the tree trunk, just four feet in front of him. "Where? I can't see him."

"I think he's dead," I say.

"Sure?" he asks.

"Think so."

"Positive? Is he breathing?" he asks.

"Wait," I whisper.

I move to the right to give Toby a clear line of fire, then take two steps closer to the downed tree. Now I can see the bear's entire body. I watch his ribs for movement. Nothing. I take my arrow off, grab my longbow by its tip, lean over the log and, with the opposite end of the bow, touch the bear's eye. He doesn't move.

"He's dead," I say. Besides, I can't hear him breathing.

# MOON

"You're right!" The banker, Frank, laughs and slaps his hand against the pile of papers on the conference table. A lot of bankers laugh and a lot of bankers slap their hands on top of the table, but there's something about this banker that's different. Not strange, not unpleasant, but different. I watch, trying to figure out what it is.

Wind-driven sleet drums against the plate glass windows. Outside, other skyscrapers are fuzzy black obelisks. Whitecaps on Lake Michigan show its sullen mood.

I look at my footprints across the custom-made carpeting that cost more than the loan I need. I feel warm air billowing from heating vents. I shiver.

"John, this deal's interesting, but it's a little small for us . . ." His eyes flash and he leans forward, something bankers never do; they always lean back in their chairs while their clients grovel forward, begging for the loan.

His lips twitch once, his hands grasp his suspenders as he leans back in the chair. His eyes cloud to anger, yet his voice remains enthusiastic. He's sending me mixed messages. I can't figure out what motivates the intensity in his voice: the tone, his desperate energy, and, lying someplace under his civilized surface, anger. It's certainly not my loan request; he's already said it's too small for the bank.

All hotshot bankers seem intense, but this guy, Frank, has an edge that transcends business. I read people well, but he's a mystery. It's a challenge to discover the driving force of that intensity. I'm intrigued.

Our business nearing its end, Frank cuts to personal matters.

"So what do you do for entertainment in central Illinois?"

Chicago people have trouble understanding life doesn't stop at the city limits. The *Chicago Tribune* derides my home county by calling it "Forgottonia." But I don't hear condescension in his voice.

"I like to hunt," I say.

"What?" He shifts in his chair as if he's uncomfortable; maybe an old injury. He seems as interested in this conversation as in our business discussion, if not more so.

"Goose season starts next weekend. I lease ground near a warmwater power-plant lake." I wait for anti-hunter rhetoric.

"I love to hunt." There's that intensity in his voice again. It's like the enthusiasm of an eight-year-old kid, that spark of energy that's hammered out of kids by fifth grade.

"Most city people don't like to hunt," I say and wonder what the heck causes his enthusiasm?

A grimace flickers across his face, and he shifts in his chair again. "I grew up on a farm in Iowa. Last fall, I hunted geese in southern Illinois, mostly snows and lesser Canadas. I didn't know they had a goose season in your area."

"Fish and Game introduced giant Canada geese to our area ten years ago. They've thrived, but now they're seriously over-populating. Our first hunting season was last year."

"I'd give anything to get a giant Canada." His intense blue eyes sparkle.

"Why don't you join me for a hunt?" I ask, wondering if it's my desire for a new business relationship that makes me invite him, or my curiosity about what's driving the guy.

Two weeks later Frank and I park under a grandfather oak at the edge of the cornfield. Pale moonbeams filter through its branches, casting irregular shadows across the pickup of my usual hunting partner, Biz Ford.

The interior light of the pickup goes on when Biz opens the door, and Coleman, his black Lab, hurtles into the night, finds my station wagon, and pees on its front tire before greeting us. His tail slams into Frank's leg, making him laugh. Even Frank's laugh has a sharp edge.

Frank and I met at three-thirty that morning at Emma's for a breakfast of biscuits and red-eye gravy and greasy coffee, but I still haven't been able to discover what makes him so interesting.

On the other hand, he didn't talk all that much at breakfast. He was fascinated at the mixture of Emma's customers: hunters clad in their down camouflage parkas and hip boots; drunks laughing, pinching the waitresses, and spilling their coffee down their shirts; other drunks, sullen, hunched two-handed over their coffee cups, mumbling prayers for a clear head and a hell-of-a-good excuse when they meet the old lady. I'll bet Frank doesn't see sights like this at the North Shore Country Club.

I tell Frank to leave his shotgun in its case and carry it plus a bulky sack of goose decoys to the blind. We stumble across rows of shin-high corn stubble that rakes loud and rough against our hunting pants. Our blind is six hundred yards ahead, in the middle of the field. The corn rows change direction, and we're able to walk in the dirt furrows between the stalks. I see moonlight glint yellow off a downed corncob lying in the dirt.

Coleman thrashes through the dried stalks looking for cripples or mice or whatever he can retrieve for Biz. Behind me, Frank heaves deep breaths. I hear him stumble. Too much time behind his fancy desk.

The blind is a four-by-eight-foot rectangle that Biz and I built from six-foot-tall cornstalks tied to steel fence posts with twine. We test the wind. It's from the west and light, so we'll place the bulk of our decoys on the east side of our blind and spread the rest between twenty and thirty yards to the west.

I show Frank how to assemble the decoys and position them as if they are feeding into the light breeze. He attacks the job with rambunctious enthusiasm. I watch his black form move through the rows of cornstalks in the moonlight; he gets most of his decoys positioned correctly. He doesn't notice when I slip behind him to straighten those that are wrong. I'm relieved.

We gather at the blind, and I watch Frank unsheathe an old Belgium Browning 12-gauge over-and-under. I'm happy it's not new. A lot of city guys talk a big game. Maybe he is a hunter. He breaks the Browning's barrel open. Biz smiles. He likes to hunt with guys who are safety conscious. I hand my shotgun to Biz, crawl into the blind, take my gun and Frank's, then he crawls in behind me. Biz repeats the process and stands to Frank's left.

I like to put a guy we haven't hunted with in the middle, between Biz and me. Things get exciting when a flock of giant Canadas set their wings and swing into the spread of decoys. When the shooting starts, many inexperienced hunters concentrate so hard on the geese that they swing wildly and sometimes don't see the hunter at their side. As a result, hunters have lost their heads.

So when the geese swing close and we rise to shoot, Biz and I lean into the guy in the middle so he can't swing the barrel toward us.

We watch the full moon set in the west and the sun, fiery bright, rise in the east, and we watch flocks of ducks and geese on the horizon, but they don't come close enough to call. We tell stories, look at our watches, talk about the geese and the ducks and the deer and coyotes that are making comebacks in central Illinois.

Frank asks Biz about what it's like being a foreman in the forge department of the International Harvester Plow Works, and how he handles union problems and hotheads and drunks. Still there are few flights of geese and none near us. Throughout the morning, Frank acts like an enthusiastic kid, laughing and grinning and grimacing.

I look at my watch again. "Getting late. Think any more will fly?"

"Full moon screwed us. They love the moon; go out from the lake and feed and return before daylight. They're pretty well settled for the morning." River-rat wisdom. If Biz didn't have to feed his wife and two daughters, he'd be a full time river-rat, hunting and fishing all the time.

We lapse into silence, then Frank looks at me.

"There's something you should know about me."

Biz looks at me and raises his eyebrow before turning to study the horizon. I hope whatever Frank wants to say isn't personal, like a confession, or worse. While I'm intrigued by the guy, I hope this won't turn out to be some sort of big-city personal thing; something that would embarrass Biz, who needs a lot of time with a fellow before letting him get close. I suck in my breath.

"Yeah? What should we know, Frank?"

"I don't get much warning, so when I've got to go, I've got to go right away. I don't want you boys to be embarrassed."

"Huh?" I see Biz frown.

"Got cancer."

"Oh." What the hell do I say now? I look at Biz for help. He studies the horizon real hard.

"Terminal."

"How long you had it?" I look for a flock of geese. There aren't any, but I still can't look at Frank.

"Six years, six operations. Doc told me I was a dead man after the first operation six years ago. They tell me that every year, but I've beaten them. There's not a lot of my insides left to take out. It's inside me, eating my guts out. The docs tell me it's my anger at the damned cancer that's kept me alive. They fly me all over the country to speak to cancer victims."

I sensed anger lying under the surface during our meeting at the bank, but his enthusiasm overwhelms his anger; he's still a mystery. I look past Frank at Biz, who is a statue staring into space.

I finally look at Frank. "You don't seem angry, at least on the surface. How does the cancer affect you?"

"It's funny. Things that used to seem so important now don't mean a damn. It's the little moment-to-moment things of life, like being here with you guys waiting for a flock of geese, that are so precious."

That's it! That's what I'd seen, but couldn't recognize in Frank's personality. It is so simple, so . . .

"Gotta go!" Frank shoves past Biz, dives out of the blind, and runs toward the oak trees but stops in the middle of the decoys and drops his pants. In an act of kindness, he turns toward us before squatting.

We turn and look east, pretending to scan the horizon. Behind us, Frank moans. I sneak a glance at Biz, and I see something I've never seen before . . . tears.

Biz clears his throat. "Jeeze, he's taking a dump in the middle of our spread. Poor bastard. What're we going to do?"

"Well, when we pick up our decoys, we'd better step real careful."

Biz grins, then we hear something else between Frank's grunts . . . a honking flock of geese, close. Biz and I duck down, grab our shotguns and peek through openings in the cornstalks. High above Frank, a flock of twenty giant Canadas tumble down toward the decoys. In an effort to cover Frank's moans, I start honking on my goose call.

Squatting, Frank looks over his shoulder, then starts a bare-ass duck waddle toward the blind for his shotgun, but he's seized again and his moans join the wild honking of the geese. They set their wings and float directly above Frank, who falls onto his knees and elbows, ass up, thinking the geese won't see him in the middle of the decoys. The lead goose drops his neck straight down and stares at Frank.

Biz has a grin on his face. I'm embarrassed about my laughter.

We jump up and unload at the geese. Three thump in the corn rows near Frank, who has his nose buried in the dirt. His hands cover his head, and his white ass is still high in the air.

Coleman bursts out of the blind and drags the nearest goose back. We try not to laugh, but it's impossible. Frank looks at us, face blackened with dirt, teeth white, and he's laughing, too. Thank

God. He stands up, pulls up his pants, and retrieves the other two geese.

"Man, that's the most fun I've had in a long time," he says. His eyes are bright, and he jumps from foot to foot.

Biz studies him for a long moment, puts his hand on Frank's shoulder and says, "Frank, you're a hell of a man. You're the first hunter in history to moon a goose."

# RUNAWAYS

"Here's where our horses jumped the fence." My hunting buddy, Nic Patrick, stands in the middle of the creek and points to a huge flat boulder where the wooden fence poles cross. There are horseshoe tracks in the mud.

"They probably ran back to that pasture next to the trail-head," I say, mentally damning the nags.

"We can spend the better part of two hunting days walking down there and bringing them back, or hope that our outfitter sees them and brings them back when he comes to pull us out," Nic says.

"Yeah, and our saddles are here, so we'd have to ride them back up here bareback. I'm sure the outfitter will bring them back," I say, trying to act confident. I'm not sure I can ride my horse bareback without falling off on a couple of the steep parts of the thirteen-mile trail.

Two days later, we're hunting above timberline on the left side of a steep valley, when Nic spots and stalks a raghorn bull elk. The distance is deceptive, the bull is farther than Nic thinks, and his arrow hits the bull's right rear hoof. The bull dashes down the open slope to the creek, then up the other slope that's cut by five vertical strips of timber. Each ribbon of pines, separated by a quarter-mile of grassy slope, is about two hundred yards wide by a half-mile long. The bull, limping now, disappears into the timber.

"He'll bed down in the heavy timber. I'll climb to the top of that boulder and spot for you," I say.

Nic follows the bull to the creek and disappears into the trees. At that instant, the bull sneaks out of the top and trots across the open slope to hide in the next strip of trees.

Nic tracks the bull to the top of the trees, then walks out into the open, loses his tracks, and using his binoculars, looks at me. I stand up, extend my arm, and point to the next band of trees. Nic creeps across the open slope and disappears into those trees. The instant he enters the top of that ribbon of pines, the bull sneaks out the bottom and sprints across the open grass slope to hide in the next group of trees.

The chase lasts all day, from one group of trees to another, until the bull wins the deadly game of hide and seek.

That night in our tent, Nic says, "I hate wounding an animal."

"That bull will be fine, Nic. You just nicked his hoof. No worse than a cut finger. Maybe we'll find him in the morning," I say.

"Yeah, but we don't have a heck of a lot of time to hunt. The outfitter will be here right after lunch to pick us up," Nic says in a flat monotone.

"Sure hope he brings our horses," I say, dreading a long walk to the trailhead.

At dawn, we're hunting for the bull three miles above our camp in the strips of dark timber where the bull gave Nic the runaround. Four frustrating hours later, standing near the creek that cuts the two slopes, we decide it's time to get back to camp to pack up for the outfitter.

"I'll hunt back to camp on this side," I say.

"I'll take the trail on the other side; it'll be quicker. I'll have an omelet ready for lunch by the time you get back. We can pack after we eat," Nic says.

I work through the strips of timber, then follow a game trail out of the high country through heavy timber toward our camp. The sun is bright and warm. I stop, take off my heavy camouflaged shirt, tie it on my pack, then follow the game trail down through the pines.

Near the bluff where the trail dives into the creek, about a half mile above our camp, I see the sun glinting off something white . . . an elk antler. It looks like the raghorn bull Nic hit yesterday.

I nock an arrow and judge the distance; twenty-five yards. The bull springs out of his bed and runs, I draw and loosen an arrow. It disappears into the bull's side.

I find the bull at the bottom of the bluff, next to the creek. He has a small cut just above his right rear hoof. I smile. Nic will be happy, too.

I gut out the elk and walk back to camp to have lunch with Nic, who thinks I'm kidding when I mention I'd shot his bull. We hike back to the elk, quarter and prepare him for packing out, then return to camp and gather our gear.

"I'm exhausted. I sure hope the outfitter brings our riding horses," I say, slumping down on a log next to my saddle.

We hear horses trailing up the narrow valley and watch the outfitter lead his packstring into camp. I don't see our saddle horses.

The outfitter reins his horse to a halt, leans on his saddle horn and asks, "Git anything?"

"Yeah, we shot a bull this morning. But our horses jumped the fence a couple days ago and headed down valley. Did you see them?" I ask.

"Nope. Didn't see any horses," he says.

"What're we going to do?" I ask.

He laughs. "I've got just enough horses to pack your gear and that elk. Looks like you're gonna walk out."

We walk out.

# WEREN'T IT SWELL?

"Want one of those?" The outfitter points to his home movie screen, where two world-record-class bighorn rams feed on a mountainside.

"Isn't that what we're going to be hunting tomorrow?" I say.

He laughs. "Naw, those are special rams. One of those would cost you ten thousand."

He's hinting about something illegal. I won't get sucked into his plot, so I don't respond. I've heard about guys like this. The word "crook" crosses my mind, but it's too late to get out of this hunt. He's got my money, and I won't get it back. We're going sheep hunting.

The next day our packstring leaves from Daisy Pass. His other clients, Mexican newlyweds, ride ahead of me. I wonder how the Mexican is going to meet his goal of killing all of North America's four species of sheep, a grand slam, on his

217

honeymoon. It's hard enough to have one successful hunt for one species.

Crossing a river, the mule that carries my sleeping bag falls into a hole and the current sweeps him downstream. He finds his footing and scrambles out, sopping wet.

"How about stopping to check if our equipment is dry?" I ask the outfitter, hoping that my bag is dry.

"Don't have time. Gotta make it over the pass before it gets dark," he shouts.

Rain falls, then turns to snow. Hours later we're forced to stop by a blizzard. The outfitter and his son put up a tent for the honeymooners and a large tarp for the rest of us. Snow howls in one end of the tarp and blows out the other.

I attempt to pull my sleeping bag out of its cover. It's frozen. I vow that next time I'm going to wrap my bag inside a plastic garbage bag. It's going to be a very long night, sitting by the fire.

The cook shivers by the fire, looking like he's been abducted from a tavern. He grimaces and looks startled. His head pivots, eyes staring at the wall of snowflakes, and he realizes he's hunkered next to a sputtering fire and not sitting on a bar stool.

The outfitter walks over and asks him, "Well, Cookie, what's for dinner?"

"Any damned thing you can heat up." Cookie points to the unopened panniers, the horsepacking boxes that carry our food and kitchen supplies.

The next day we retreat to the base camp at Daisy Pass. After the weather clears, the outfitter takes his son and me on horses across a mountain pass to set up a spike tent.

"Now you stay off that ridge. Don't skyline yourself," he says over and over again to his son, Ronnie.

The next morning is clear and warm and I leave my rain jacket in camp. We're at the north end of the mountain, about three hours from our spike camp, when another snowstorm slams into us.

"It'll be faster if we go back on the other side," Ronnie says.

The storm worsens. I'm soaked by wet snow and perspiration. We scramble down steep gullies, then climb, hand over hand, up the next side, disoriented by poor visibility.

"This is the ridge our tent's on," Ronnie assures me as he strides through the falling snow.

Forty-five minutes later he stops. "Guess it wasn't this ridge."

It takes an hour and forty-five minutes to climb back up. I begin to shiver uncontrollably. Soon I'm incoherent; I stumble and fall.

I don't remember reaching the tent, or him putting me in my sleeping bag, or sleeping close to me so my body temperature would rise.

The next morning, he brings me a cup of hot tea. "Think you can walk back to base camp?"

"Think so," I mutter.

We put our gear on backpacks and that evening stumble back into base camp, where we decide to drive down to spend the night at the Cooke City Hotel. The town, a strip of bars, motels, and filling stations cut into a high mountain valley, is soggy wet. Red neon lights reflect from oil-slick pavement. It's a depressing sight.

I'm exhausted and decline Ronnie's suggestion that we go to the bar. I go to bed. Later, I'm awakened by loud voices in the hall, then someone knocks Ronnie through the bedroom door. Arms flailing, he stumbles backward and flops over me.

"Come on," Ronnie says in a whiskey-stained voice. "Let's beat the shit out of them."

"You beat the shit out of them!" I shout. Energized, I throw him into the hallway and slam the door shut.

Ronnie sports a black eye the next day as he drives me to the airport in Billings. His brother sits in the back seat.

Ronnie shouts to his brother. "Old ladies up ahead. Let's do it!"

"Ready!" His brother says, and Ronnie pulls even, then barely ahead of the ladies' car. The woman driver does a double-take, swerves away, and slams on her brakes.

I look in our back seat. His brother is on his hands and knees with his bare ass pressed firmly against the window.

At the airport, Ronnie shakes my hand. "Weren't it a swell hunt?"

# THE MIRACLE

The September sun warms my back as I weave through jack-strawed timber on the hill above the swamp across the river from my cabin. I stop, lean my longbow against a tree, and look at my watch: quarter-to-eleven. Time to get back and do some chores.

I'm satisfied with my morning's hunt: I'm safe from three close encounters with the same cow moose and her calf. We spent the morning scaring the heck out of each other, running opposite directions around rock knobs, the swamp, and the ridge, then frightening each other on the other side. Sooner or later she'll decide I'm a threat to her baby and stomp me.

I'm happy to have stalked within twenty yards of a lone cow elk who fed on lush grass near the unused wallows. Arrow nocked, I waited for a bull to return to gather her into his harem, but there was no bull. Rut hasn't started.

I pick up my bow, step over a fallen tree, spot movement, and freeze. Thirty-five yards ahead, a sparkling stream of water, like

221

that from a five-foot-high fire hydrant, gushes out of a huge black spruce tree.

The first thing that flashes through my mind is that I'm experiencing a miracle. But I'm not all that convinced about miracles.

I raise my binoculars for a better look. Hidden from view behind the spruce, is the ass of a cow moose. I grin—it's the only time I've ever wanted to see the ass of a cow moose.

It's better than the alternative.

# WOLF GHOST

September 2, 2:30 A.M., Northwest Territories base camp.

A full bladder forces me to shuffle out of the tent. Undulating psychedelic colors steamroll toward me. I duck. Blues, greens, yellows, reds, with colors and intensity I can't describe, tumble, roll, and flash from all quadrants of the sky. It's as if I'm the magnet that draws the Northern Lights.

I creep back into the tent, where five other hunters snore, tiptoe to my cot, gather my down-filled sleeping bag, and carry it outside to the bluff overlooking the lake. I feel guilty about not sharing this with the others, but their voices would spoil nature's display.

Spreading my bag on the earth, I slip into it, lie on my back, and watch the light show. The iridescent colors roll, press down, and envelop me. I reach with both hands to scoop them up. I swear I can hear the light sizzle and can smell burnt ozone, but

223

maybe it's my imagination, overstimulated by the sight of being smothered by the Northern Lights.

They make me feel as if I'd slipped through some kind of hole in space and entered a new dimension. I've never taken drugs, but I know that no LSD trip could match this experience.

When the lights disappear just before dawn, I'm brought back to earth and time and purpose; it's the morning the plane is coming to pick us up. I'm not ready for the hunt to end.

I remember one of the hunters had killed a caribou on the mountain just above camp. Maybe there's a big black bear feeding on its carcass. The plane won't arrive until ten; there's time to make a quick hunt.

I creep back into the tent, dress in the dark, grab my bow and headlamp and sneak out of camp. The outfitter will be mad if he knows I'm hunting without a guide, but he'll be too busy to notice.

Tendrils of fog snake from the lake, misting through the beam from my headlight. One of the outfitter's horses nickers. Another answers. The game trail to the top of the mountain veers to the left. I turn off my light and am surprised it's light enough to see. The fog is backlit by the glow from the eastern sky and it seems as though I'm climbing through a magician's mist.

I stop to catch my breath and look up the mountain. The haze thins, and I can barely make out the form of a white horse standing on the trail fifty yards directly above me, watching. It looks like a stark abstract painting, spooky and spiritual.

I begin to climb; it moves forward, enveloped by the fog. I don't want to push a horse up the mountain; it'll spook a bear. I stop. The indistinct white form stops and watches me.

I have no alternative but to continue, even if he's ahead of me. I'm this far, I might as well push on. I climb. The white form moves upward.

I'm close to the top, so I stop to catch my breath. The fog turns solid white when the sun rises, then I feel a puff of breeze on my neck and watch the fog break into tendrils rushing upward to dissipate in a crystalline sky.

Standing on the top of the ridge forty yards above me, contrasted against the blue sky, is not a horse but a white arctic wolf who watches me with curious yellow eyes.

I gasp and, without raising my bow, stare back at him as if tied by a magical bond. We two predators stand, watch, and, on some level I can't explain, communicate mutual respect.

I raise my bow in a silent salute, then turn back down the trail. He deserves whatever is left of the caribou carcass. He deserves to be left in peace.

# WHERE'VE YOU BEEN?

An unformed question scratches my mind like the talons of sage-brush that claw at my bare legs. Yet the question remains as vaporous as ether. I hike across an undulating flat toward an aspen-strewn shoulder of the mountain, unable to mold the uneasy feeling into words.

I feel unbalanced without my longbow in my left hand. It's the first of June, three months away from elk season, but never too soon to get the legs in shape.

I snake around a waist-high boulder and realize that, unlike the thing that gnaws the margins of my consciousness, I can see silver leaves on gnarled sagebrush branches, feel them scuff my skin, and smell the pungent scent.

The ground rises and my fingers caress the bark of the first aspen tree. I stop, look up its trunk, and watch delicate new leaves shimmer in the breeze. If it were elk season, the leaves would be bright yellow. If it were elk season, I'd lie below this aspen and watch golden leaves dance against an infinite blue sky.

But it's not September, and my objective is to climb through the aspen groves to the slopes of Douglas fir, cut the game trail that leads to the saddle, then scramble upward to the granite mountain top.

I can't shake the feeling. Something's a bit out of kilter. A bead of sweat rolls down my forehead, down my nose, and falls, making a dark circle on my shirt five inches above my belt. Gotta stop eating so much.

Pushing through a chest-high thicket of young aspen, I become a meal for a squadron of mosquitoes. On unhinged arms, my hands flap and slap. Ignoring my hands, one mosquito follows me, insistent and arrogant. I let him land on my forehead, suck until he's slow, then I squash the son-of-a-bitch. Now there's blood on my hand and probably on my face. That was stupid; the blood will draw more of them. Hate the damned things. Frost kills the mosquitoes in elk season. Best time of year.

Still bothered by the sense that something is wrong, I climb the steep slope into a narrow, lush place. On the right, a granite cliff soars ninety feet toward heaven. I brush its surface with my fingertips and marvel at its cool smoothness. I lick the dampness off my fingers.

Each time I pass this cliff, I scan its surface for petroglyphs. I know better, yet hope that since my last visit a spirit has returned to carve pictures depicting his life. Evidence of ancients in this place would create a bridge of comprehension. It would be the last line to complete the circle. I dismiss my disappointment as being a childish fantasy. I'm too damned old for fantasies.

Trudging up the little valley, I weave through chokecherries and smell the sweet scent of water and follow its trickle to the source. It seeps from a spring a few yards below the first of the Douglas firs. It's cooler here. Heck of a good place for a grizzly bear.

That's it! My right hand grasps for the canister of pepper spray on my belt. It's not there. That's what is bothering me. Never hike without it. Too many bears. Springtime. Sow grizzlies with cubs. Mauled.

The sweat on the back of my neck turns cold. The only movement in the trees ahead is a branch that sways in a lazy breeze. I wonder if forgetting the canister of pepper spray was a senior moment or stupidity? Had to be a senior moment.

The cabin is a couple of miles behind me on the bank of the river far below. If I've come this far and haven't run into a bear, I won't. I hope.

A few minutes later, I hit the game trail that meanders through widely spaced Douglas firs. Good visibility. Won't run into anything. If I'm careful.

I remember that except for a few gnarled limber pines on the edges of the cliff, the summit is bare. Why would a griz be up there? No food. Nothing but some big slabs of broken rock, so I can't get surprised.

The trail, worn through the pine needles to bare dirt by migrating elk, steepens. Panting, I lean against the trunk of a fir that is so large two men couldn't get their arms around it. Its rough bark presses against my sweating back. I sniff, wishing the fir had the sweet vanilla scent of the ponderosa pines of Colorado.

The trail weaves through downed timber in the narrow saddle. A jagged cliff looms on the left. I cut to the right and climb away from the trees. The Vibram soles of my boots clutch smooth granite as I make my way to the top.

Relieved that I haven't run across a bear, I feel safe and stop to look at the 360-degree view. The river valley ends at Pilot Peak, a Matterhorn-shaped peak that John Colter of the Lewis and Clark expedition named for his navigational marker. Farther to the right, the snowcapped Beartooth Mountains sparkle against a blue sky. Wooded pockets, sagebrush benches, and cliffs complete the view.

I decide to walk to the west edge of the cliff to rest and soak up the view. Halfway there, a small slab of granite shifts and grinds under my foot.

Thirty yards in front of me, on the far side of a rock ledge, I hear a noise. Then, just above its granite shelf, I see a hairy hump rushing to the left. Toward me. The thing I fear most.

I look for a tree. To the right. Twenty, maybe thirty yards. On the edge of the cliff. Tall enough. If I make it.

I remember author Tom McNamee telling me that you can't outrun a griz. "Your best defense is to lock your fingers at the back of your neck, drop to a fetal position on your elbows and knees, and pray it's a sow. Don't fight back and, for God's sake, don't scream, because that will only excite her. Don't let her get at your front side, your face, and good stuff."

I've been told that she'll bat you around, tear your scalp off, and bite your thigh, but once satisfied you're harmless, she'll walk a few yards away and watch. You'll be okay if you don't moan or thrash around. If you do, she'll come back to maul you until she's convinced you won't threaten her young.

And I've heard that if you're attacked by a boar, you might as well run like hell. When he hits you, fight like hell. Otherwise you're lunch.

No one has determined how to tell the difference between a sow and boar when six hundred pounds of enraged bear is charging.

These thoughts take a nanosecond. As I spin toward the tree, the hairy hump grows larger. Ears flat against her skull, a cow moose scrambles over the rock ledge and charges. At that moment I forget grizzlies as I am consumed by fear of moose.

I run flat out toward the tree. Her hooves strike the granite behind me, gaining fast. I tuck my skinny ass under me and give it all I've got. The rhythm of her hoofbeats change. I glance over my shoulder. Her right hoof slashes the air just inches from my back.

In a desperate act to swat her away, I grab the bill of my baseball cap and swing it behind me. I hook the tree trunk, whirl to the cliff side, and scramble up through the branches. My cap covers her nose. She slams it on the ground, rears high, and with front legs stiff, she stomps and stomps and stomps. My guts squeeze tight.

Halfway up the limber pine, a small branch breaks under my foot. She spots me and charges. I scramble to the top branch. She rears and her hooves flail at the branch and strike inches below my feet. I can't climb higher. My sweat turns sour.

She hammers the tree. The branch I'm standing on shakes. My body shakes.

I break off a dead branch to whop her on the end of the nose. She really gets pissed. I hold onto the tree. She backs up and tries to jump up to knock me down with her hooves. She's a lousy jumper. Thank God.

I strip off my sweaty tee shirt, and hoping man-stink will drive her away, I throw it at her head. She stomps it into shreds. Then she looks up at me and rears. With her hooves flailing, she drums the trunk of the tree. It sways. I look over my shoulder and down a three-hundred-foot cliff into a jumble of car-sized boulders. If the tree falls, no one will find my body.

Like chunks of rock exploding from a volcano, my surface values vanish. There remains only one core value, the will to survive. My mind grasps it as tightly as I grasp the trunk of the tree.

The moose stops, looks at me with angry black eyes, then turns, trots off, and disappears behind the rock ledge. She must have left her newborn calf there.

I wait for another attack. Nothing. I have both arms wrapped around the trunk of the pine. A true tree-hugger.

Fifteen minutes later, I'm convinced that she's gone. Maybe found a way down the other side. I feel the crotch of my walking shorts. Dry. "Scared shitless" is true. When you're scared, really scared, your sphincter muscle tightens. I smile and begin to climb down, wondering how I got up through the jumble of branches. My left toe touches the ground and the dead branch I hold onto with my right hand snaps.

Here she comes again! She charges, I scramble back up the tree.

She's striking the trunk of the tree, trying to shake me out so she can stomp me good and proper. I wrap my arms and legs around branches and the tree trunk. She tires, disappears behind the rock. Thirty minutes later I try again. She charges again.

She retreats behind the ledge. I look down at my ranch far below. I can make out my wife, Tish, walking from the corral to the barn. I whistle. Maybe she'll hear me, get the binoculars, see my predicament, load the shotgun with slugs, saddle a horse and ride around the back side of the mountain, shoot the damned moose, and save me.

She doesn't hear me, but the moose does and charges again.

A quiet hour and ten minutes later, I sneak out of the tree, run like hell twenty yards to the next one and scramble up twelve feet. No moose. Ten minutes later, I creep down and run as fast as I can and climb the next tree, thirty-two yards away. Counting steps as I run keeps my mind off the image of a hoof impaled in the middle of my back.

No moose.

Forty-five minutes later, shirtless, scratched, with spots of pine sap and dried blood on my arms and chest, I stumble into the barn. Tish is standing at the workbench oiling a saddle. She hears my footsteps behind her and without looking says, "Where've you been?"

# CHALLENGED AGAIN

"How do you feel about John's birthday party?" Tish asks when I carry groceries into the kitchen of our cabin.

"Great party, but having a forty-year-old kid makes me feel ancient." I place a sack of Idaho Reds in the potato drawer.

Tish points out the window toward the meadow across the river. "There's your bull!"

I grab the binoculars that hang from a nail next to the door, trip over a chair, and rush to the window. There he is! The same bull elk that got me so excited last year that I put my boxer shorts on backwards. I smile.

"There's plenty of daylight left. Aren't you going after him?" Tish asks without taking her eyes from her binoculars.

"It's too late to hunt. I'll just watch him this evening," I say.

His antler tips are polished ivory. I count seven points on each side, a wide spread, a world-class trophy.

"He survived," I say, imagining how he avoided hunters during last year's rifle season.

"I'm glad the wolves didn't kill him," Tish says.

"Or that he didn't starve to death in the winter snow," I reply.

The huge-bodied bull struts stiff-legged around the edge of his harem, eight cow elk and three calves. He lifts his head, lays his antlers against his back, and bugles a challenge. I crack open the door to hear the scream from the bull that tantalized me all last season, the bull that romps through my imagination every night.

I've hunted him without success the first part of this bow season, scoured every hidy-hole in the valley. Now he shows up in the meadow across the river. It's almost like he's challenging me.

He did the same thing last year. I know it's a coincidence, that animals don't think like humans, don't play games, don't issue deadly challenges. Yet I'm convinced he and I are connected by some sort of bond.

We watch him until dark, then I sharpen arrows, lay out my camouflaged hunting clothes, hip boots, hat, and bugle. I fill a bottle of water and put cheese and gorp in ziplock bags and stuff them into my pack.

"Guess it's time to go to bed," I say.

"It's only seven-thirty, John."

"Yeah, but I need to get up early." I grin as I sprint up the split-log stairs to our bedroom where I plan to open the double doors to listen to him scream all night.

Tish sits in the old rocker next to the fireplace, knitting. The fire crackles, and its yellow light makes the shadows dance. She laughs. "You're as excited as our grandchildren on Christmas Eve."

"Better than Christmas . . . whole lot better," I mutter while unbuttoning my shirt.

I rise at five, dress in the dark, and slip out of the cabin to stand on the river bank to listen for his scream. An owl hoots, the river tumbles over boulders, but there is no scream. I feel a puff of breeze on my neck, shiver and tug at the collar of my camo shirt. Streaks of pink lighten the eastern sky when I lift my elk call to bugle. He'll answer a challenge if he's near.

The owl answers over the babble of the river, but the bull is silent. My chest constricts with disappointment. I should have blasted out of the cabin last night to hunt him. He's pulled a disappearing act.

I walk toward Lake Creek, then stop next to the buck-and-rail fence and give a half-hearted bugle. He screams back. I see his yellow body slip through dark lodgepoles on the far side of the river. Crouching next to the fence so he won't see me, I wait and watch. One of his cows steps out of the trees and begins to feed in the meadow.

I feel the feather-touch of air on the left side of my face and realize that the elk are going to feed downwind through the open meadow toward their bedding ground. I can set up an ambush. I sprint back toward the cabin, slide down the river bank, and ease into its cold water. Careful not to make splashing sounds that would alert the elk, I wade the river, take off my hip boots, and put on my camo sneakers. Then I crawl up the bank on my belly, crawl through frosty grass, and kneel under the overhanging limbs of a spruce tree and wait.

I bugle a challenge. He screams an answer from halfway up the timbered hillside. His cows are feeding in the meadow, closer now. I nock an arrow and rest my longbow on the tip of the lower limb to minimize the movement of drawing my arrow.

The bull moves through the trees on the hillside, screams, and rakes the underbrush with his massive antlers. He walks down to the buck-and-rail fence at meadow's edge and vaults over. A three-foot-wide yellow bush dangles from his right antler. He circles his cows, who continue to feed. He's too far for a shot.

The bush hanging from his antler is a testament to his physical power. I can't rip a bush like that out of the ground. The wooden stick I call my bow becomes insignificant. I'm insignificant.

Wisps of his vaporized breath drift upward, a stark contrast to the dark pines. He shakes his head with violence, sending the yellow bush tumbling. Then he lifts his head and bellows another challenge. I remain silent, kneeling fifty yards away.

A calf stares at me, becomes curious, and walks toward me. The bull licks the butt of a cow who scoots out of his way, telling him she's not ready to mate.

The calf looks at me, sniffs the air, then walks closer. A few more steps and it'll figure out I don't belong in the meadow and give the alarm. I hope the vapor of my breath is not visible and hold my breath when the calf looks directly at me. My stomach muscles tighten.

The bull spots the calf straying from his harem and trots over to herd it back. The calf spins and runs back to join the cow elk. The bull stands broadside between twenty-five and thirty yards away. He's looking straight ahead, at the trees at the far end of the meadow. A perfect shot.

My right elbow creeps back to pull the shaft toward full draw. The bull's head snaps toward me. Body rigid, he stares. I try to hold my longbow at full draw without shaking, try to hold my breath so he doesn't spot the telltale vapor of a predator. He's got to look away . . . got to, or he'll dodge my arrow. He won't. I can't hold. I can do the ethical thing: let down and spook him, or I can let the arrow go and hope his eyesight is bad. In an act of desperation, I release the string and my arrow jumps forward.

He sees the tip of my bow move and dips to gather himself for a leap forward as my arrow flies a foot over his shoulder. He jumps, then trots thirty yards and stops. The bull turns broadside to look at me, then looks at his harem retreating down the meadow. The rising sun spotlights his antlers as he throws his head back to utter a final scream. The tips of his antlers touch his butt. The breeze carries his musky scent. He turns and follows his cows into the trees, then follows them up the hillside.

I finally rise on shaking legs to return to the cabin.

During the last four days of bow season I see him three more times, but he doesn't let me get close, won't answer my bugle.

The night before rifle season Tish asks, "Are you going to shoot your bull in the morning?"

"Maybe, I haven't decided." I look at the .338 Winchester Magnum hanging on my wall and wonder. I'm torn. A lot of other hunters have heard the rumor of this bull and will be hunting for him. How will I feel if someone else shoots an animal I've been hunting for years? A bull elk with which I feel a special bond. Would I be jealous? If I were to take my rifle off the wall in the morning and shoot him, would I be acting out of greed?

I open the door next to the bed and get under the covers and listen for his scream. There's nothing but hollow silence above the rippling river. I hate to think I'll never again hear his scream.

The blankets are too hot, so I toss them off. I listen, get cold, and pull the blankets over me again. I visualize all the times I've hunted the bull. The time last season, when the rising sun spotlighted him standing seventy yards away in the swamp, challenging me with his screams.

I remember my feelings when he dipped his head, drove his ivory-tipped antlers into the ground, and threw a wheelbarrow load of dirt and yellow swamp grass over his shoulder. And, after he ran off, I recall sitting on the hillside across the river from my cabin, warmed by the sun, and thinking it had been another great hunt.

I look at the hands of the clock creeping toward dawn and the time for my decision; will I hunt him with my rifle? The clock says four-thirty and I remember the countless nights during the past year that I thought about that bull, wondered what he was doing, anticipated seeing him again, anticipated the challenge of hunting for him once more.

I think we're both getting old, that each has fewer years ahead of him than behind him. I decide not to use my rifle. I make a mental date to bow-hunt him again next year, then pray to the Great Spirit to guide this bull through rifle season, winter snows, and the wolves so we can meet again.

The next morning I'm at the corral feeding the horses when I hear the shot.

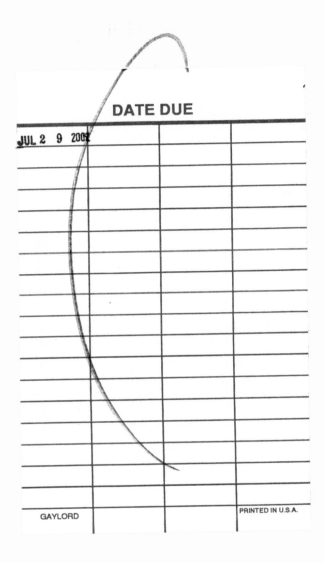